3-D GEOMETRIC ORIGAMI
MODULAR POLYHEDRA

RONA GURKEWITZ
AND
BENNETT ARNSTEIN

DOVER PUBLICATIONS, INC.
NEW YORK

This work was supported by a Connecticut State University/American Association of University Professors Research Grant 1993–1994.

Bibliographical Note

3-D Geometric Origami: Modular Polyhedra is a new work, first published by Dover Publications, Inc., in 1995.
All drawings are by Bennett Arnstein; photography by Bill Quinnell.

Library of Congress Cataloging-in-Publication Data

Gurkewitz, Rona.
    3-D geometric origami : modular polyhedra / Rona Gurkewitz and Bennett Arnstein.
        p.   cm.
    ISBN 0-486-28863-3 (pbk.)
    1. Origami.   I. Arnstein, Bennett.   II. Title.
TT870.G87   1995
736′.982—dc20   95-9545
                                                                        CIP

Manufactured in the United States of America
Dover Publications, Inc., 31 East 2nd Street, Mineola, N.Y. 11501

Table of Contents

Introduction

This book contains diagrams for constructing over 50 three-dimensional modular origami models based on various polyhedral forms. Also included are background material and explanations of how to assemble the models. The modules are for the most part simple, while the assembly of the modules is generally "low intermediate" in difficulty.

Modular or unit origami is constructed from more than one piece of paper. The pieces of paper that make up one model are usually folded identically. The modules interlock and stay together by a system of "pockets" and "points," explained later, requiring the help of tape or glue only in exceptional instances. The process of constructing modular origami is like the working of an elegant puzzle, the end product being a work of art. To heighten the artistic element, folders can select paper of various kinds and colors from which to construct their models.

Two features of this book that are original are: 1) an attempt to enumerate the models that can be made from different numbers of a given module; 2) the use of various starting shapes, or bases, for modules that have related folding sequences. We think of these two directions as helpful to seeing "systems" of modules and models. The model we find most interesting is a truncated hexadecahedron which we call "The Egg" (see pages 7, 37 and 64). It is made from 48 one-piece triangular modules. We feel this model is unusual because it is modular, yet ovoid instead of spherical.

The authors owe a debt of gratitude to the pioneers of this field: Lewis Simon, Bob Neale, Jack Skillman and Sonobe. The first three started designing models in the early 1960s, Skillman being credited as the first American modular origami designer.

RONA GURKEWITZ

Part One
Background Material

Super Spike Ball, page 43

What Is a Polyhedron?

Put simply, a polyhedron is a three-dimensional figure made up of sides called faces, each face being a polygon. A polygon, in turn, is a two-dimensional figure made up of line segments, called edges, that are connected two at a time at their endpoints. In a polyhedron, several polygonal faces meet at a corner (vertex). When all the edges of the polygon are of equal length the polygon is called regular. An equilateral triangle and a square are examples of regular polygons made up of three and four edges respectively. A cube is a polyhedron with six square faces.

Polyhedra related to the models in this book are the Platonics, the Archimedeans, the Kepler-Poinsot and some miscellaneous ones. Consider the Platonics. There are five of them, so named because they were known at the time of Plato (427?–347 B.C.). These polyhedra are also called regular polyhedra because they are made up of faces that are all the same regular polygon. The five Platonic polyhedra are the tetrahedron, the cube, the octahedron, the dodecahedron and the icosahedron. The tetrahedron is made from four equilateral triangles. The cube is made from six squares. The octahedron is made from eight equilateral triangles. Less familiar are the dodecahedron and the icosahedron. The dodecahedron is made from 12 regular pentagons with three meeting at each of 20 corners (vertices). The icosahedron is made from twenty equilateral triangles with five triangles meeting at each of 12 corners. The Platonics and the other polyhedra related to the origami models in this book are pictured and described in the pages immediately following.

Illustrations and Facts about Polyhedra

Platonic Solids

Name: **Tetrahedron**
No. of faces: 4
Shape of faces: equilateral triangle
No. of edges: 6
No. of corners: 4
No. of edges or faces meeting at each corner: 3

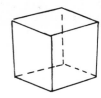

Name: **Cube**
No. of faces: 6
Shape of faces: square
No. of edges: 12
No. of corners: 8
No. of edges or faces meeting at each corner: 3

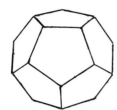

Name: **Octahedron**
No. of faces: 8
Shape of faces: equilateral triangle
No. of edges: 12
No. of corners: 6
No. of edges or faces meeting at each corner: 4

Name: **Dodecahedron**
No. of faces: 12
Shape of faces: pentagon
No. of edges: 30
No. of corners: 20
No. of edges or faces meeting at each corner: 3

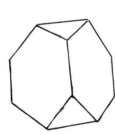

Name: **Icosahedron**
No. of faces: 20
Shape of faces: equilateral triangle
No. of edges: 30
No. of corners: 12
No. of edges or faces meeting at each corner: 5

Archimedean Solids

Name: **Truncated Tetrahedron**
No. of faces: 8
Shape of faces: 4 hexagon, 4 equilateral triangle
No. of edges: 18
No. of corners: 12
No. of edges meeting at each corner: 3
No. of faces meeting at each corner: 2 hexagon,
   1 equilateral triangle

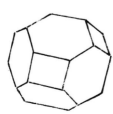

Name: **Cuboctahedron**
No. of faces: 14
Shape of faces: 6 square, 8 equilateral triangle
No. of edges: 24
No. of corners: 12
No. of edges meeting at each corner: 4
No. of faces meeting at each corner: 2 square, 2 triangle

Name: **Truncated Octahedron**
No. of faces: 14
Shape of faces: 8 hexagon, 6 square
No. of edges: 36
No. of corners: 24
No. of edges meeting at each corner: 3
No. of faces meeting at each corner: 2 hexagon, 1 square

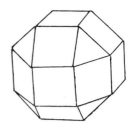

Name: **Rhombicuboctahedron**
No. of faces: 26
Shape of faces: 18 square, 8 equilateral triangle
No. of edges: 48
No. of corners: 24
No. of edges meeting at each corner: 4
No. of faces meeting at each corner: 3 square, 1 triangle

Name: **Snub Cube**
No. of faces: 38
Shape of faces: 6 square, 32 equilateral triangle
No. of edges: 60
No. of corners: 24
No. of edges meeting at each corner: 5
No. of faces meeting at each corner: 1 square, 4 triangle

Name: **Snub Dodecahedron**
No. of faces: 92
Shape of faces: 12 pentagon, 80 equilateral triangle
No. of edges: 150
No. of corners: 60
No. of edges meeting at each corner: 5
No. of faces meeting at each corner: 4 triangle, 1 pentagon

Name: **Truncated Icosahedron**
No. of faces: 32
Shape of faces: 20 hexagon, 12 pentagon
No. of edges: 90
No. of corners: 60
No. of edges meeting at each corner: 3
No. of faces meeting at each corner: 2 hexagon, 1 pentagon

Kepler-Poinsot Solids

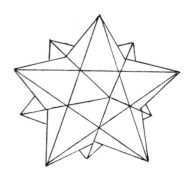

Name: **Stellated Dodecahedron 1**
No. of points: 12
No. of faces to point: 5

Name: **Stellated Dodecahedron 2**
No. of points: 20
No. of faces to point: 3

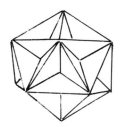

Name: **Great Dodecahedron**
No. of external points: 12
No. of internal points: 20

Miscellaneous Solids

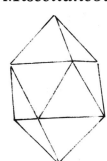

Name: **Hexadecahedron**
No. of faces: 16
Shape of faces: equilateral triangle
No. of edges: 24
No. of corners: 10
No. of edges or faces meeting at each corner: 4 at north pole
  or south pole, 5 at the other eight corners

Name: **Equilateral Triangle Dodecahedron or Double Diamond Hexahedron**
No. of faces: 12 triangles or 6 diamonds
Shape of faces: 12 equilateral triangle or 6 double triangle
  diamond
No. of edges: 18 on dodecahedron; 12 on hexahedron
No. of corners: 8
No. of edges or faces meeting at each corner: dodecahedron:
  3 at north pole or south pole, 5 at other six corners;
  hexahedron: 3

Name: **Truncated Hexadecahedron or "The Egg"**
No. of faces: 26
Shape of faces: 16 hexagon, 8 pentagon, 2 square
No. of edges: 72
No. of corners: 48
No. of edges meeting at each corner: 3
No. of faces meeting at each corner: 2 hexagon and 1 square
  at eight polar corners, 2 hexagon and 1 pentagon at the
  other forty corners

Note: The pentagon faces are slightly warped when the solid is made from 16 hexagon modules. Both hexagons and pentagons are warped when the solid is made from 48 triangle modules at the corners.

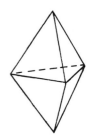

Name: **Double Tetrahedron**
No. of faces: 6
Shape of faces: equilateral triangle
No. of edges: 9
No. of corners: 5
No. of edges or faces meeting at each corner: 3 at north pole
   or south pole, 4 at the other three corners

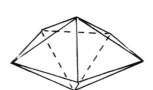

Name: **Double Pentagonal Pyramid**
No. of faces: 10
Shape of faces: equilateral triangle
No. of edges: 15
No. of corners: 7
No. of edges or faces meeting at each corner: 5 at north pole
   or south pole, 4 at the other five corners

Polyhedra:
Connections with Different Fields

Though polyhedra are considered mathematical objects, they find application in many other areas besides math. These areas include art, architecture, astronomy, biology, chemistry and crystallography.

Art: The very popular work of M. C. Escher utilizes different polyhedra such as the dodecahedron.

Architecture: The geodesic domes of Buckminster Fuller influenced later buildings that were built in geometric shapes based on polyhedra.

Astronomy: In the 16th century Johannes Kepler used the Platonic polyhedra as the basis for his theory of how the planets orbited the sun.

Biology: Some viruses have coats that are shaped like icosahedra. Also, radiolaria look like stellated polyhedra with lots of points.

Chemistry: The molecular structures of some substances are modeled in the shape of polyhedra. For example, methane can be viewed as a tetrahedron. Fullerene is made up of sixty carbon atoms arranged as on the corners of a truncated icosahedron which is roughly the shape of a soccer ball.

Crystallography: Many crystals take the shape of polyhedra. For example, fluorite is octahedral; sugar, gold and copper are cubic.

Part Two
Making Models

(Clockwise)
Dodecahedron Flower Ball, page 39
Great dodecahedron (from Pentagon modules, page 58)
Great dodecahedron (from Simplified Pentagon modules, page 60)

Using the Diagrams and Directions

Overview

In using the diagrams for a model you should first familiarize yourself with the underlying polyhedra. Next you should familiarize yourself with the Definition of Symbols, which describes the meanings of the symbols used in the diagrams. These two steps are important but one can always repeat them by referring back to the appropriate pages when working on a model.

A word of warning often heard at origami conferences is "Don't get in over your head." It makes sense to try easier models first and build up to the more difficult ones. But there will always be those who are impatient and want to proceed differently. They should be prepared to retrace their steps.

If you have not folded modular origami before, you can expect that when there are several models that can be constructed from different numbers of modules, it is generally easier to construct the models made from fewer pieces. Also, modules may be related in that they use a similar folding sequence, but a different starting shape. It is interesting to fold these models one after the other to see the relationships between them. Usually the names of the modules indicate a relationship between them.

Reading and Following the Diagrams

Origami diagrams have a language of their own and everybody needs practice when reading a new language. One hint for reading a diagram is to look at the step you are working on, try to do what is shown and then look at the next step to see if what you have folded has been done correctly. If it has been done correctly it will match what is shown in the next step.

When reading a step of a diagram you must pay careful attention to all of the information in the step. This includes every mark on the paper. If you are unfamiliar with a symbol, look it up in the Definition of Symbols section. Often several folds are indicated in one diagram step to save space. Be sure you understand all of them. Time spent carefully reading a diagram pays off in less time spent refolding your model. (On the other hand, lots of new models have been created by accidental variations on other models.)

What is *not* shown in the diagrams is that one often must often "fiddle" with the paper (that is, mold and manipulate it somewhat improvisationally, according to necessity), especially with the last few modules of a model. One may have to partially unfold a module in order to insert a point into a pocket. This process is strange at first, but can be mastered. It is this process of assembling the last few modules of a model that makes many models "intermediate" in difficulty. The difficulty of assembly may be intermediate even though the difficulty of folding the individual modules is simple.

Definition of Symbols

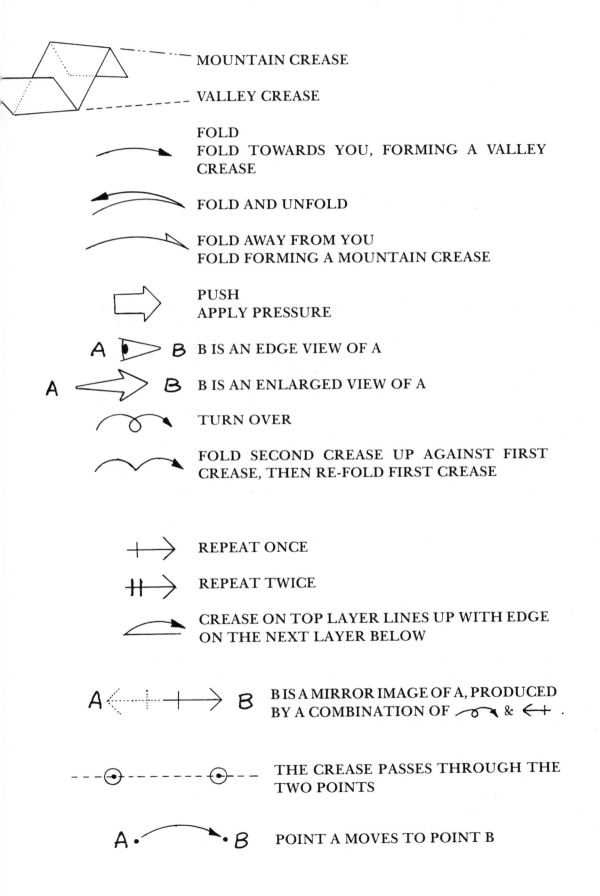

MOUNTAIN CREASE

VALLEY CREASE

FOLD
FOLD TOWARDS YOU, FORMING A VALLEY CREASE

FOLD AND UNFOLD

FOLD AWAY FROM YOU
FOLD FORMING A MOUNTAIN CREASE

PUSH
APPLY PRESSURE

A ▷ B   B IS AN EDGE VIEW OF A

A ⟹ B   B IS AN ENLARGED VIEW OF A

TURN OVER

FOLD SECOND CREASE UP AGAINST FIRST CREASE, THEN RE-FOLD FIRST CREASE

REPEAT ONCE

REPEAT TWICE

CREASE ON TOP LAYER LINES UP WITH EDGE ON THE NEXT LAYER BELOW

A ⟷ B   B IS A MIRROR IMAGE OF A, PRODUCED BY A COMBINATION OF ↶ & ↤ .

THE CREASE PASSES THROUGH THE TWO POINTS

A•   •B   POINT A MOVES TO POINT B

11

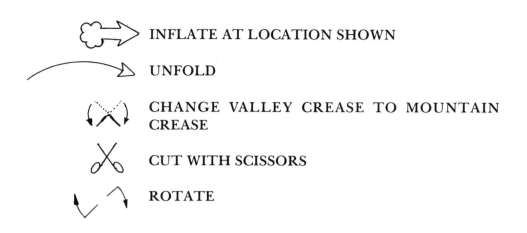

INFLATE AT LOCATION SHOWN

UNFOLD

CHANGE VALLEY CREASE TO MOUNTAIN
CREASE

CUT WITH SCISSORS

ROTATE

The Assembly Process

Overview

There are various methods for folding and assembling modular origami. One
can fold *all* of the pieces before assembling them, or one can install each piece
into the model as soon as it is folded. When adding a module, there may be many
sites where it can fit into the partially finished model and so an additional level of
systematization can be devoted to deciding where to put the module. For
example, one might try to put modules together in groups of three and then put
the groups together. I find this style more difficult than having a model "grow"
piece by piece.

Another consideration which affects the assembly process is the desired paper
and color scheme of the final model. Some people like their models colored as
symmetrically as possible with no two pieces of the same color touching. Other
choices include using all pieces of the same color; or *most* pieces of the same color
with another color thrown in at random here and there. It is interesting to try
different colorings for the models as a great deal of the aesthetic impact of a model
depends on the colors used in its construction.

Locking Modules Together

There are many different techniques used to "lock" origami modules together.
By locking two modules together, we mean folding them so they will not come
apart easily. To those unfamiliar with the modular style of origami, this process
sounds awkward, impossible or certainly difficult compared to using glue or tape
to hold the modules together. Modular origami enthusiasts of course find the
ingenuity involved in locking pieces together aesthetically pleasing. It is also
often neater to lock than use tape or glue.

In this book the main type of lock used is what we call the Point and Pocket
lock. In this lock one module supplies a point and a second module supplies a
pocket for the point to be inserted into. Usually the assembled point and pocket
are refolded in some way that holds the model together. In the diagrams, dotted
lines may be used to indicate where a point is to be inserted into a pocket. The
dotted line shows that the point goes under a piece of paper that makes up the
pocket.

Creating Your Own Models

When it comes to creating polyhedral based models there are some heuristics that can be used. One thing to do is to try to put together different numbers of modules. When diagrams teach you a modular fold they usually show you a module and one model that can be made using the module. Often other models are possible using different numbers of modules.

When trying to enumerate the models possible from a given module, use pictures of polyhedra as a reference. Pay attention to things like how many modules can meet at a corner and what is the basic shape of a module or group of modules. For example, if we are working with a triangular module we look for polyhedra with triangular faces and then see how many modules are needed and how they can be connected. After a while, we get to know the polyhedra shapes by heart, because we have been looking at them so closely. We have found that modules are usually part of an edge, face or vertex of a polyhedra.

Another tack is to start with a different shape of paper and try to follow the same steps used previously in a module. For example, if you bring two edges together with a square, try doing the same thing with a triangle. This is a suggestion for experimentation, though, and it does not always produce a new module. We have used the idea in developing many modules in this book and have tried to indicate which modules are related by using similar names.

Part Three
Preliminary Constructions

(Clockwise)
Stellated dodecahedron (from Equilateral Triangle Strip modules, page 48)
Tetrahedron (from Triangle Edge modules, page 53)
Stellated octahedron (from Equilateral Triangle Strip modules, page 48)
Stellated dodecahedron (from Equilateral Triangle Strip modules, page 48)

Equilateral Triangles

How to Make Equilateral Triangles by Bennett Arnstein

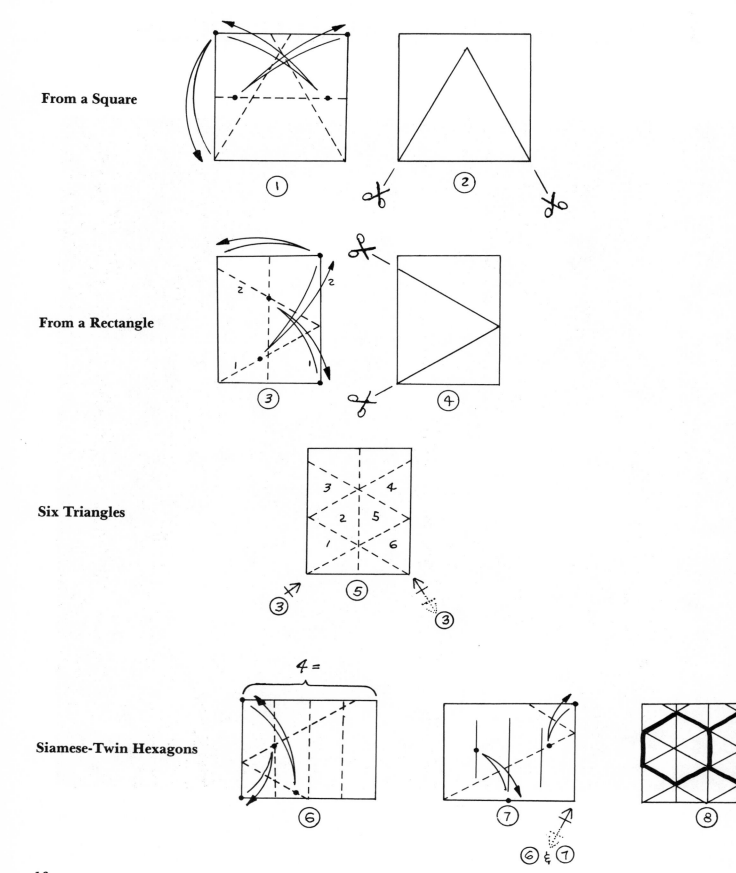

From a Square

From a Rectangle

Six Triangles

Siamese-Twin Hexagons

How to Make 20 Equilateral Triangles from a Square or *28 Equilateral Triangles from an 8½″ × 11″ Rectangle*

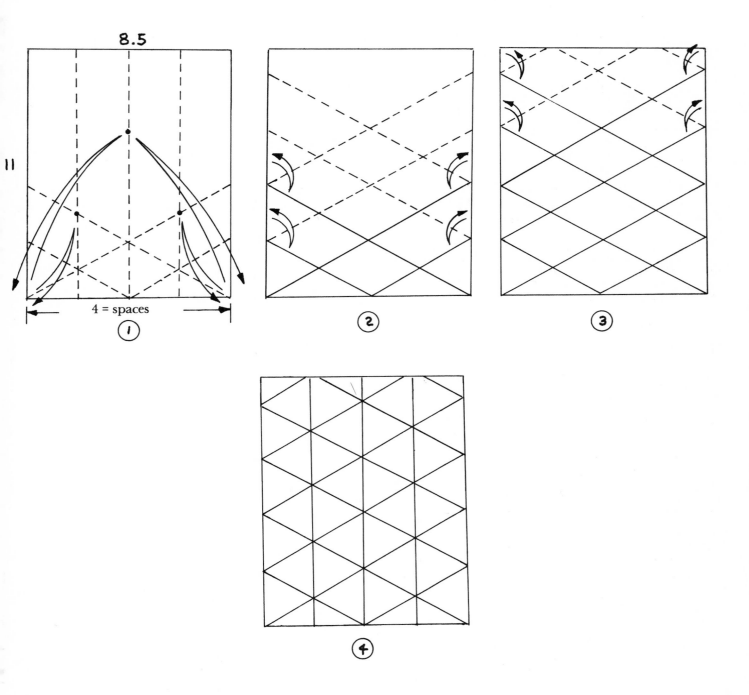

altitude of triangle = short side of rectangle ÷ 4

Equilateral Triangle Tessellation for Snub Cube Flat Pattern
by Bennett Arnstein

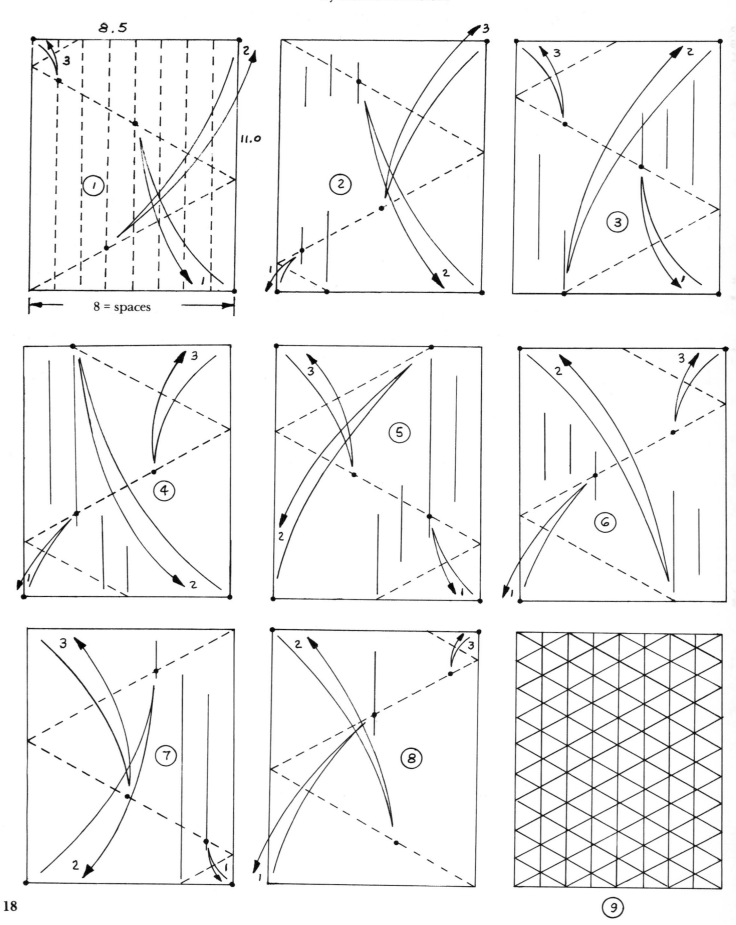

Equilateral Triangle Tessellation for Snub Dodecahedron
Flat Pattern by Bennett Arnstein

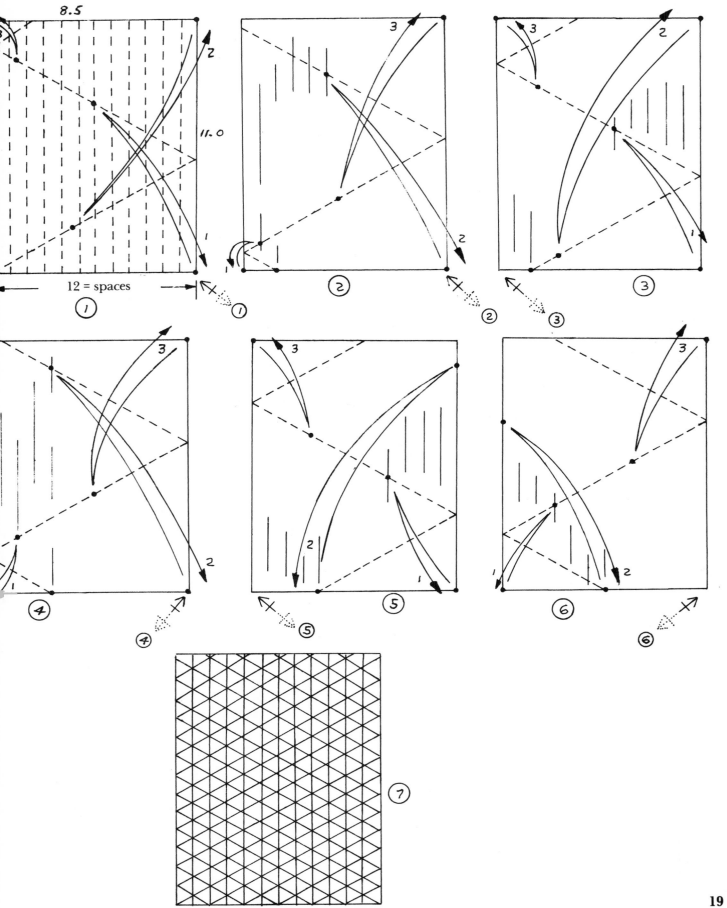

Pentagons

How to Fold a Pentagon from a Square

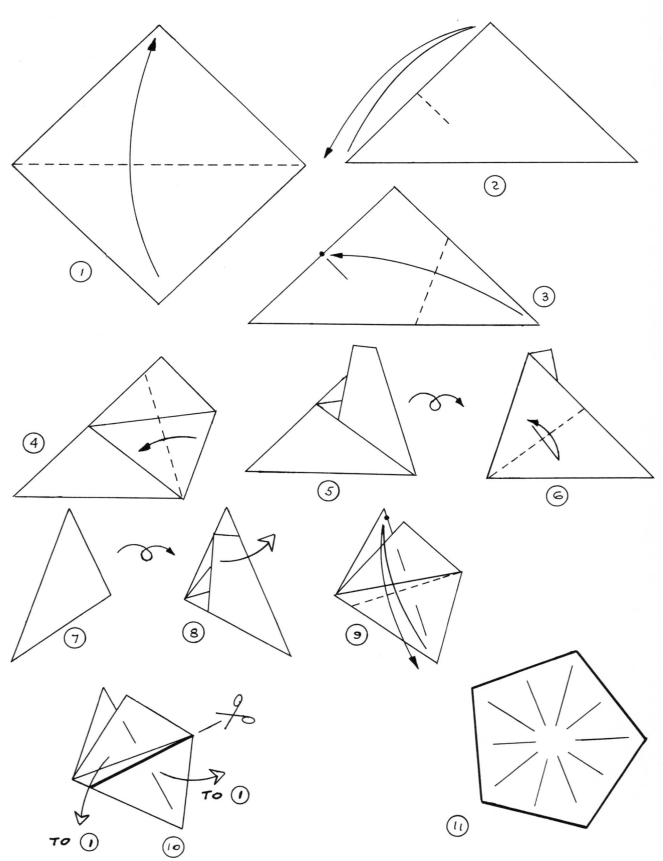

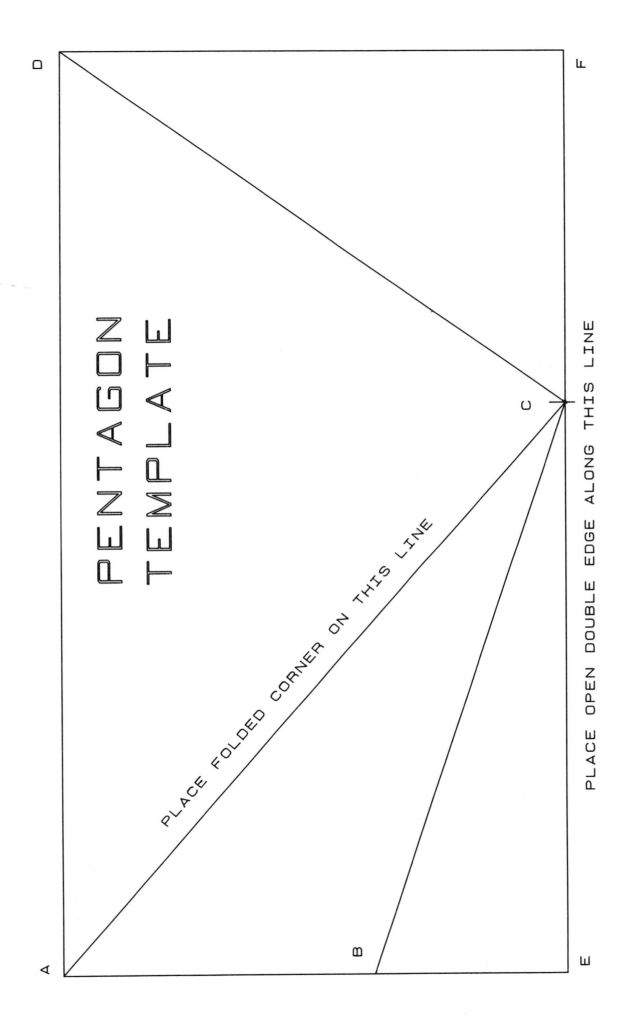

PENTAGON TEMPLATE

PLACE FOLDED CORNER ON THIS LINE

PLACE OPEN DOUBLE EDGE ALONG THIS LINE

21

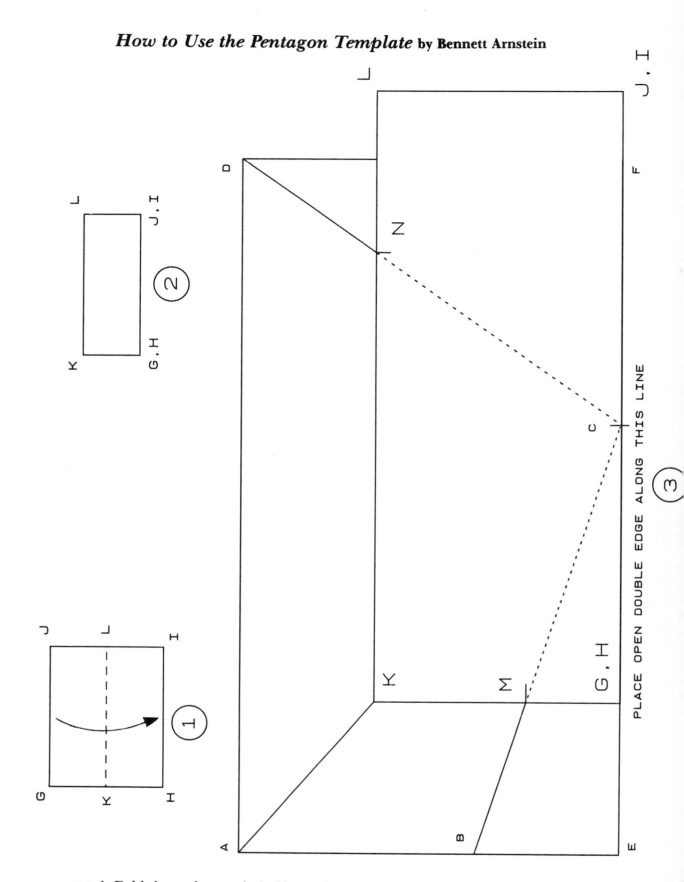

FIG. 1: Fold sheet of paper in half to arrive at FIG. 2. FIG. 3: Slide the folded sheet along line EF on the template until the folded corner K lies in line AC. Mark points M, C, and N on the folded sheet and draw lines MC and CN using a ruler. With a pair of sharp scissors cut lines MC and CN through both layers of the folded sheet. The pentagon, folded in half, is KMCN.

Hexagons

How to Make Hexagons by Bennett Arnstein

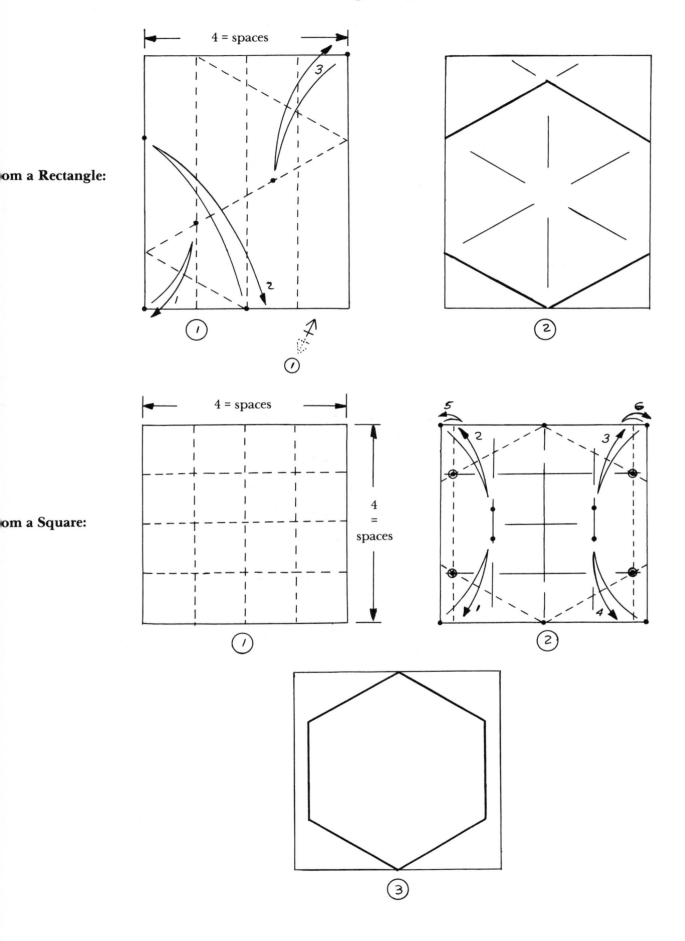

From a Rectangle:

From a Square:

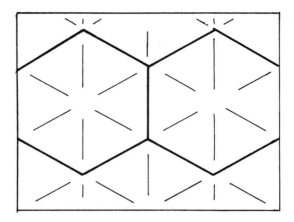

One set of Siamese-Twin hexagons from a rectangle folded to make 16 equilateral triangles

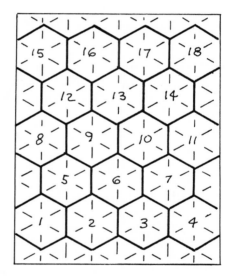

Eighteen hexagons from a rectangle folded to make an equilateral triangle tessellation for a snub cube flat pattern

How to Fold a Square or Rectangle into Three Equal Parts
by Lewis Simon & Terry Hall

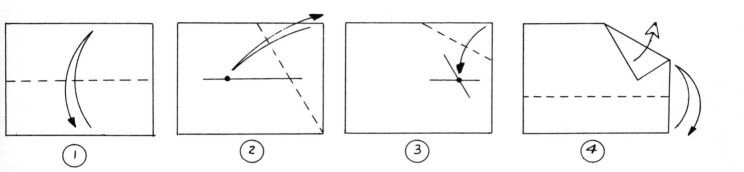

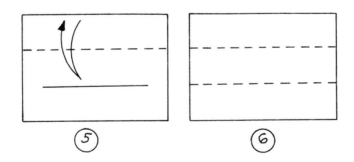

Part Four
Diagrams of Models

(Above) Icosahedron
(Below) Octahedron
(Both composed of Triangle Edge modules, page 53)

Simple Constructions to Try First

Inflatable Irregular Octahedron **by Bob Voelker**

Colored side up

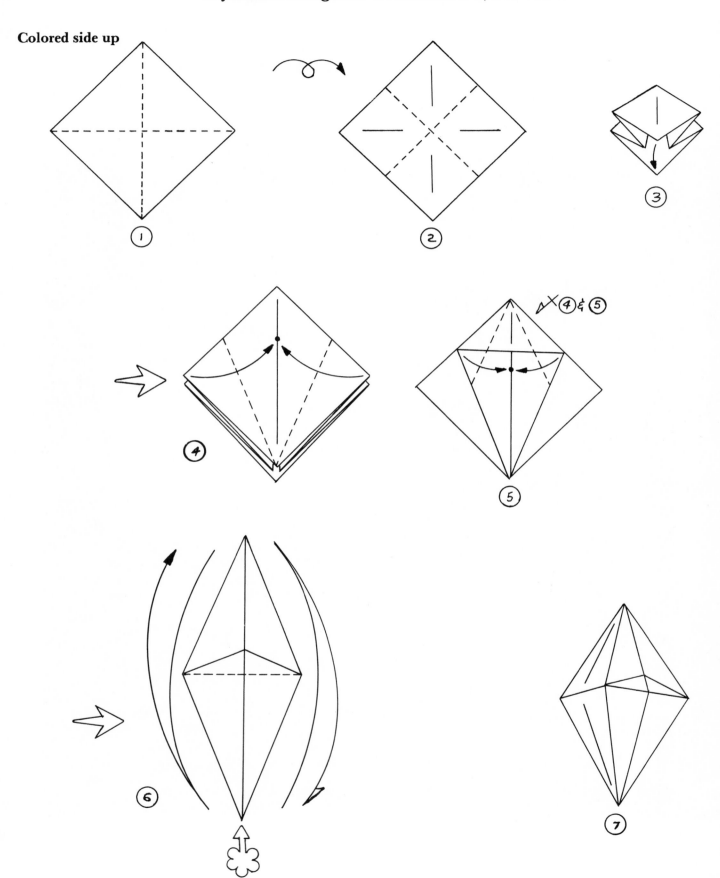

Puzzle Cube by Bob Neale

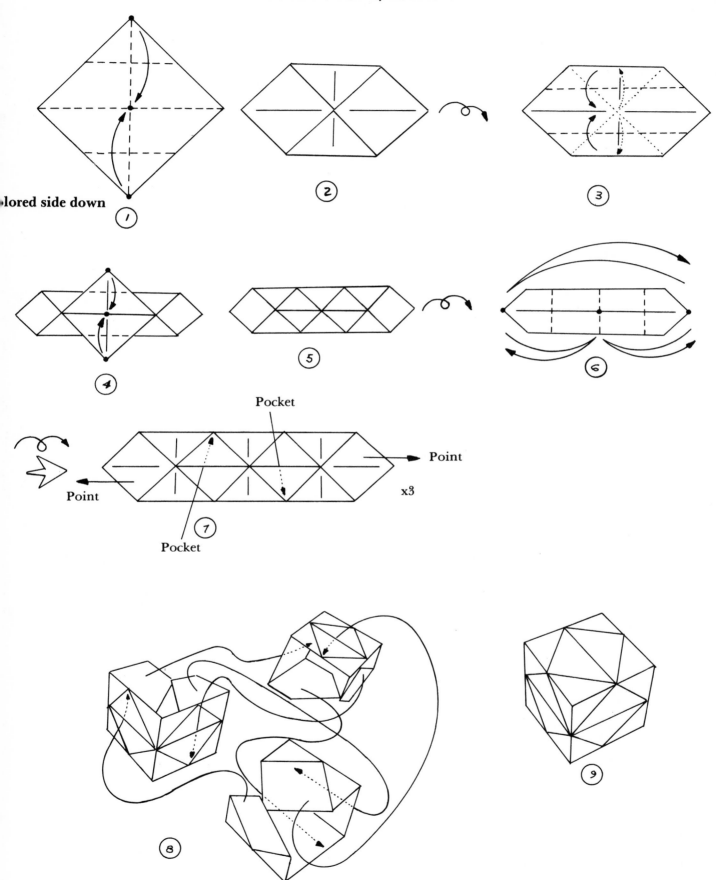

colored side down

① ② ③

④ ⑤ ⑥

Pocket

Point

Point

Pocket

x3

⑦

⑧ ⑨

Tetrahedron from Siamese-Twin Hexagons by Rona Gurkewitz

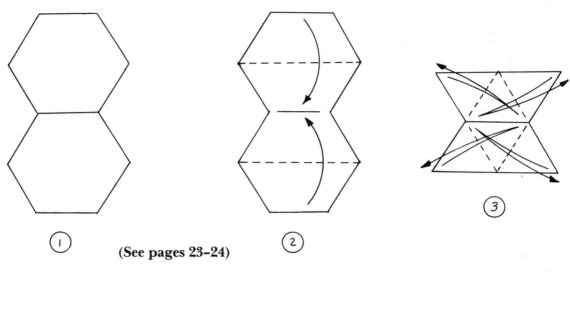

(See pages 23–24)

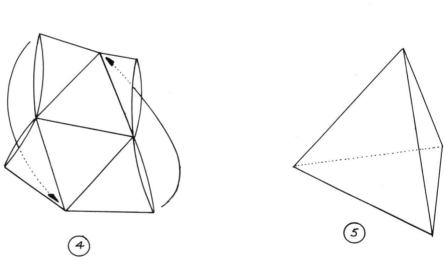

Two-Piece Octahedron Skeleton by Bennett Arnstein

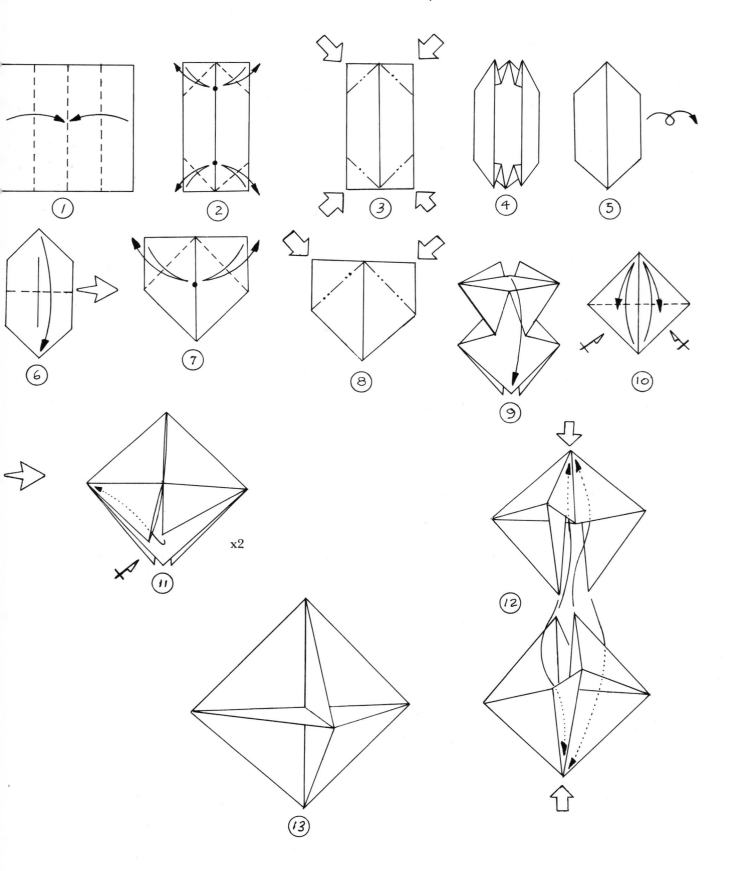

Truncated Tetrahedron from Hexagons by Rona Gurkewitz

Start with eight hexagons. Four will be hexagon faces and four will be triangular faces.

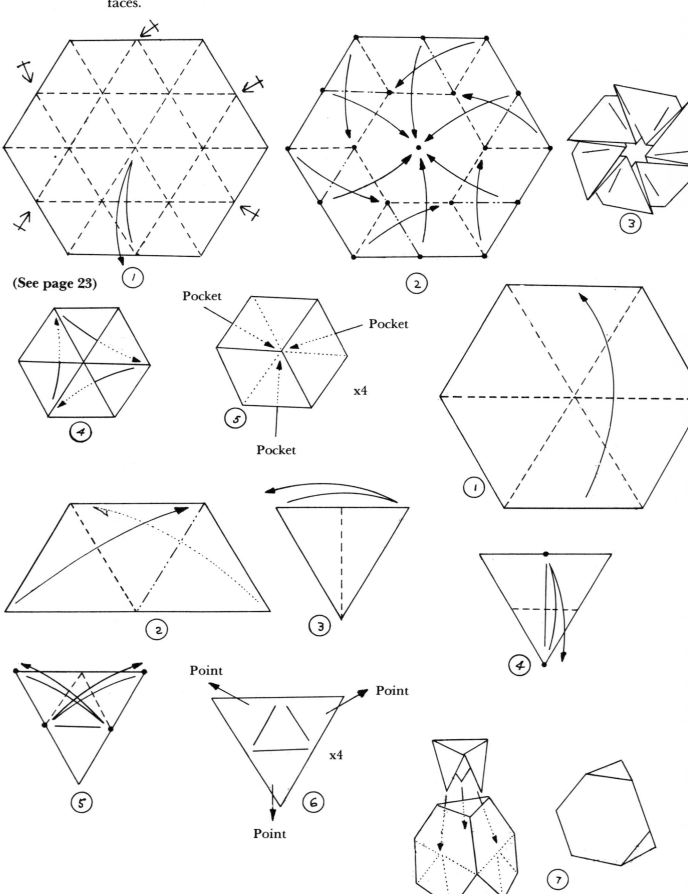

(See page 23)

Pocket

Pocket

Pocket

x4

Point

Point

Point

x4

Eight-Sided Module: Truncated Cube by Rona Gurkewitz

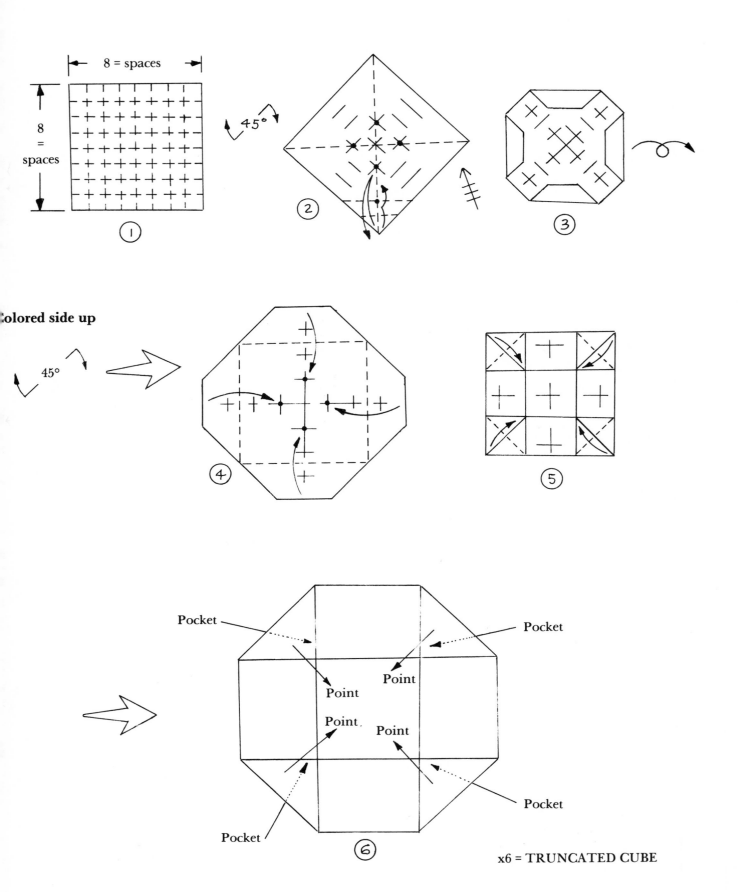

8 = spaces

8 = spaces

45°

Colored side up

45°

Pocket — Pocket

Pocket — Pocket

Point

Point

Point

Point

Pocket

Pocket

x6 = TRUNCATED CUBE

Flat Unit System

Square Module Flat Unit: Small Rhombicuboctahedron
by Rona Gurkewitz

Module of Japanese origin

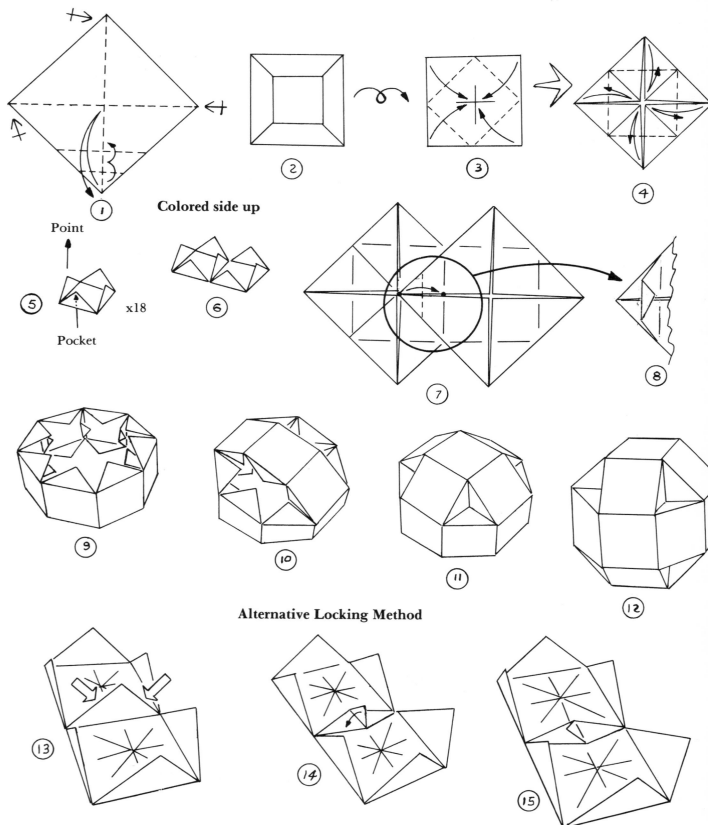

Point

Pocket

x18

Colored side up

Alternative Locking Method

Hexagon Module from a Triangle
by Bennett Arnstein and Rona Gurkewitz

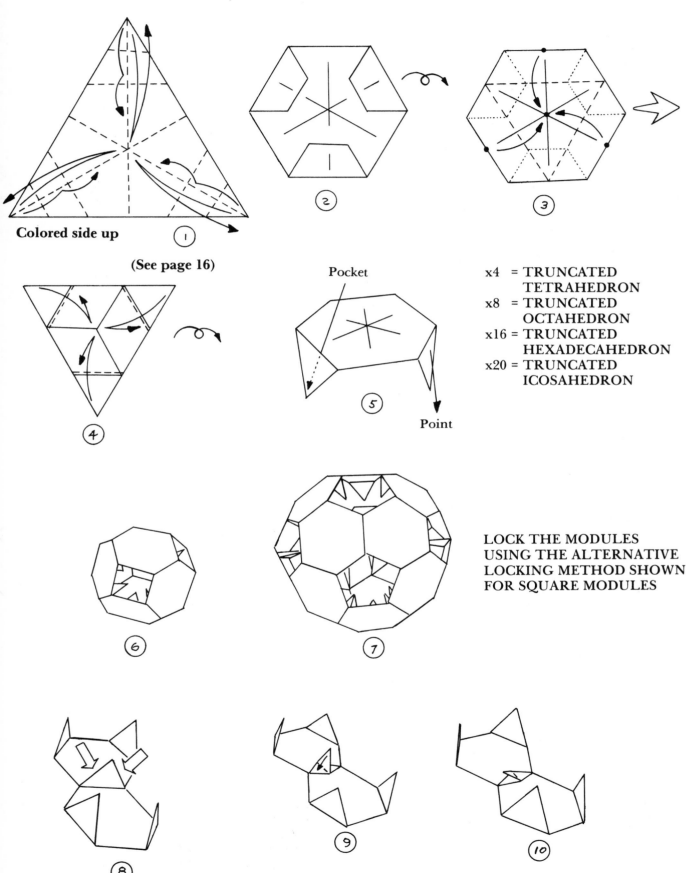

Colored side up

①

(See page 16)

②

③

④

Pocket

⑤

Point

x4 = TRUNCATED
        TETRAHEDRON
x8 = TRUNCATED
        OCTAHEDRON
x16 = TRUNCATED
        HEXADECAHEDRON
x20 = TRUNCATED
        ICOSAHEDRON

⑥

⑦

**LOCK THE MODULES
USING THE ALTERNATIVE
LOCKING METHOD SHOWN
FOR SQUARE MODULES**

⑧

⑨

⑩

Triangle Module from a Hexagon
by Rona Gurkewitz and Bennett Arnstein

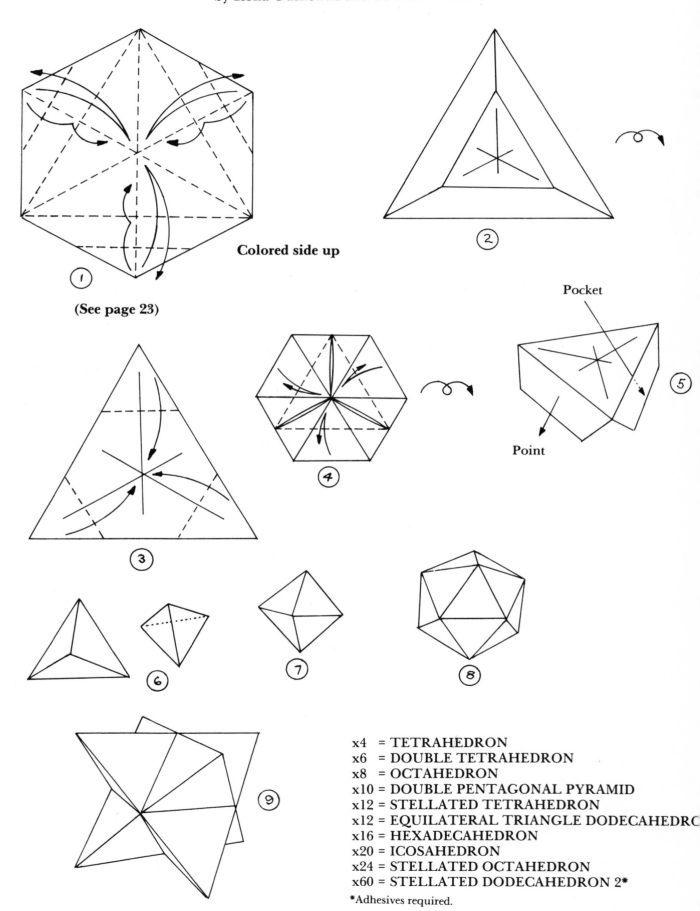

Colored side up

(See page 23)

Pocket

Point

x4 = TETRAHEDRON
x6 = DOUBLE TETRAHEDRON
x8 = OCTAHEDRON
x10 = DOUBLE PENTAGONAL PYRAMID
x12 = STELLATED TETRAHEDRON
x12 = EQUILATERAL TRIANGLE DODECAHEDRO
x16 = HEXADECAHEDRON
x20 = ICOSAHEDRON
x24 = STELLATED OCTAHEDRON
x60 = STELLATED DODECAHEDRON 2*

*Adhesives required.

One-Piece Module System

One-Piece Triangle Module by Bennett Arnstein

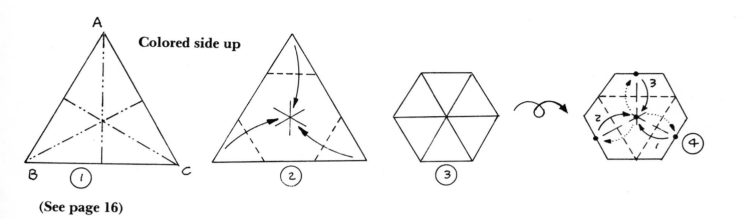

Colored side up

(See page 16)

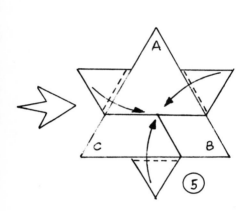

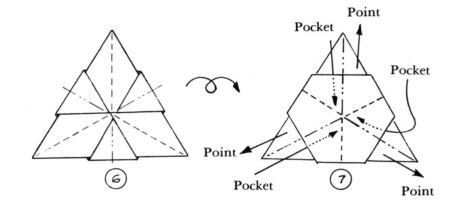

Pocket

Point

Pocket

Pocket

Point

Point

Pocket

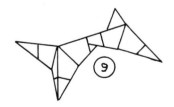

x12 = TRUNCATED TETRAHEDRON
x20 = DODECAHEDRON
x24 = TRUNCATED OCTAHEDRON
x48 = TRUNCATED HEXADECAHEDRON
x60 = TRUNCATED ICOSAHEDRON

One-Piece Square Module by Bennett Arnstein

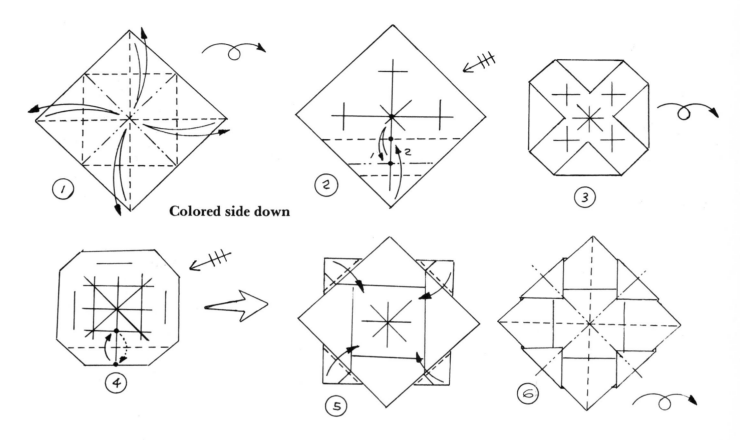

Colored side down

① ② ③

④ ⑤ ⑥

x6 = OCTAHEDRON SKELETON
       (USE SQUARES 6″ OR LARGER
x12 = CUBOCTAHEDRON
x24 = RHOMBICUBOCTAHEDRON

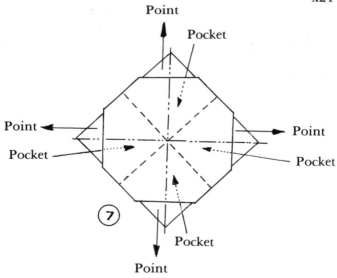

Point

Pocket

Point

Pocket

Point

Pocket

Pocket

⑦

Point

Simple Dodecahedron Systems
Dodecahedron Flower Ball
by Bennett Arnstein and Rona Gurkewitz

Triangle module based on Rona Gurkewitz's Spike Ball module (page 42)

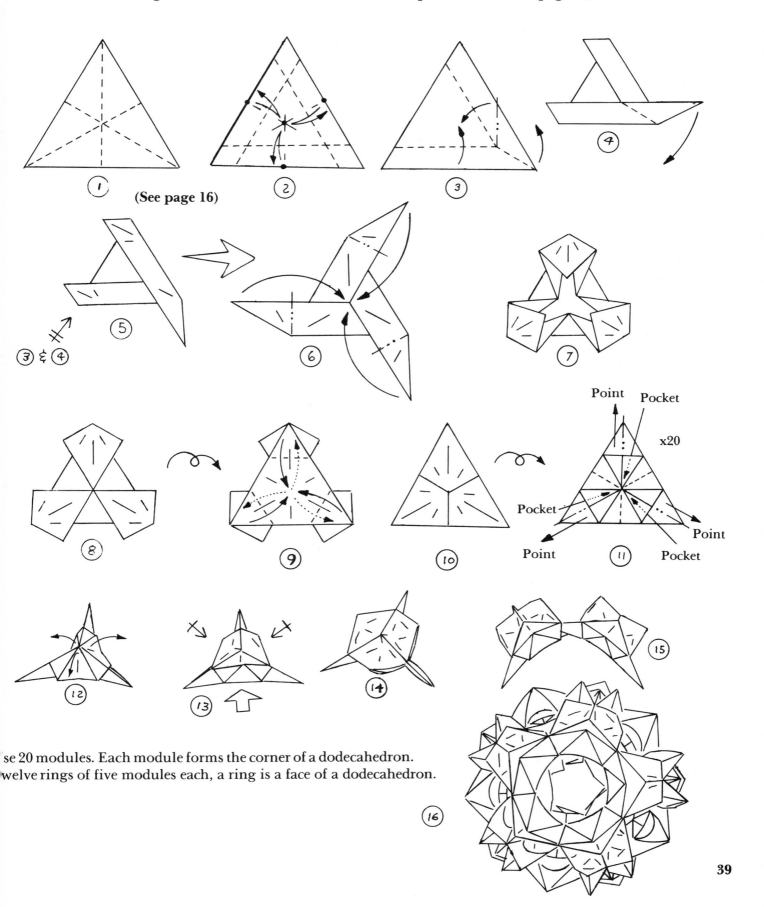

(See page 16)

Point   Pocket

x20

Pocket

Point   Point

Point   Pocket

'se 20 modules. Each module forms the corner of a dodecahedron.
'welve rings of five modules each, a ring is a face of a dodecahedron.

Modular Dimpled Dodecahedron Ball by Rona Gurkewitz, Module by Lewis Simon, Connector by Rona Gurkewitz

You will need 60 modules and 30 connectors to make the ball. Six-inch squares make a ball about nine inches high. If model is to be handled, glue is recommended.

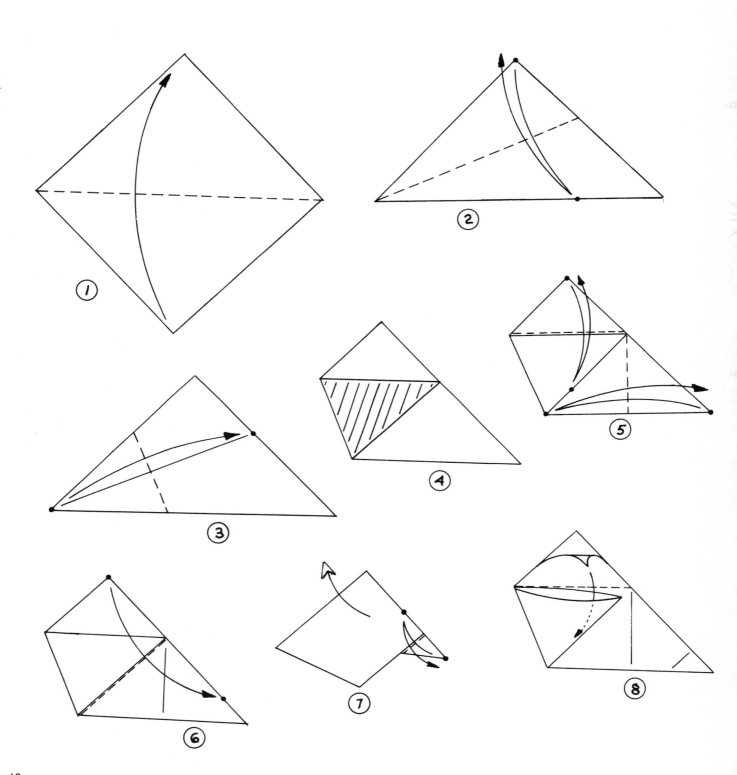

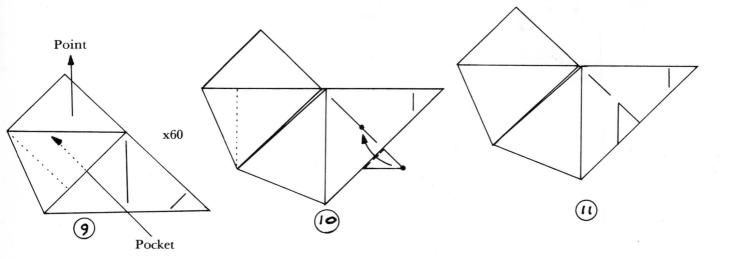

Point

x60

Pocket

⑨　　　⑩　　　⑪

nnector

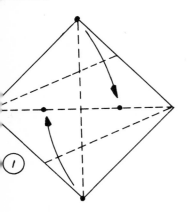

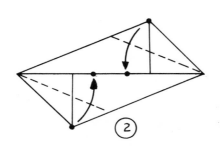

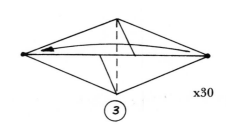

x30

①　　　②　　　③

embly

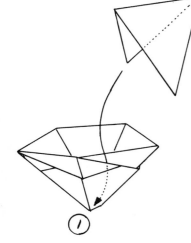

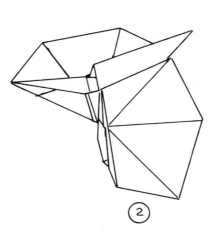

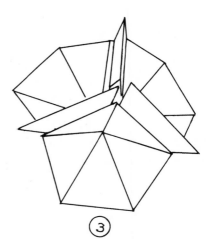

①　　　②　　　③

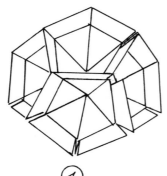

④

Cuboctahedron Systems

Spike Ball Module by Rona Gurkewitz

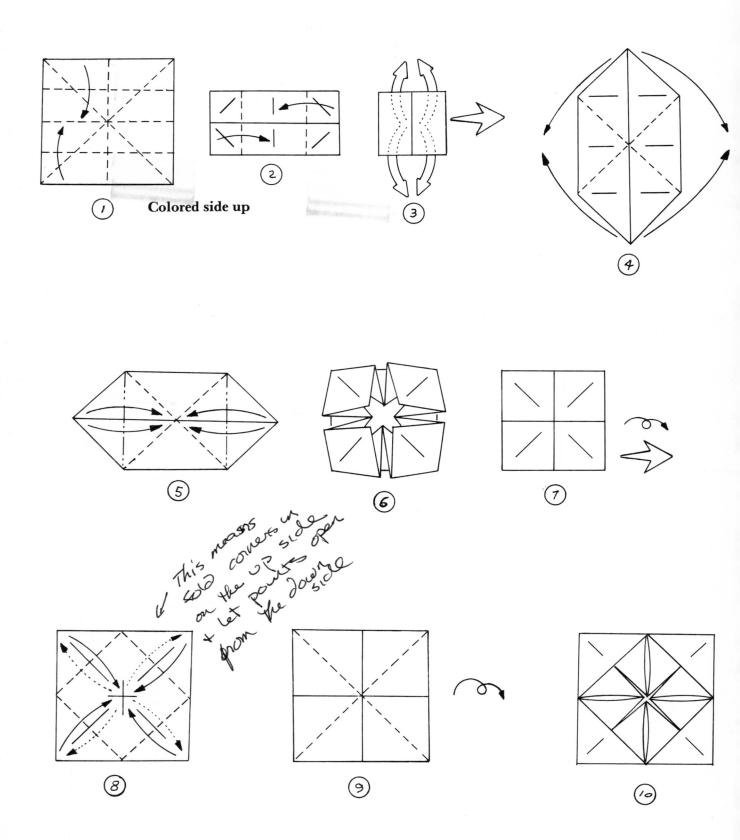

Colored side up

This means fold corners in on the UP side & let points open from the down side

Spike Ball and Super Spike Ball
by Rona Gurkewitz and Bennett Arnstein

Use Spike Ball Modules (see previous diagram).
x12 = SPIKE BALL (Cuboctahedron based)
x24 = SUPER SPIKE BALL (Rhombicuboctahedron based)

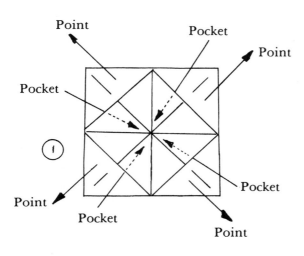

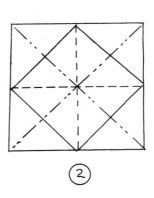

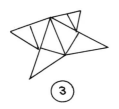

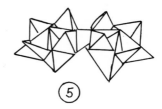

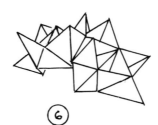

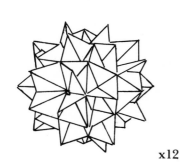

x12

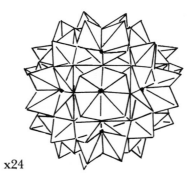

x24

Ornamental Ball Module by Rona Gurkewitz,
Assembly by Rona Gurkewitz and Bennett Arnstein

Fold the center points of the Spike Ball Module (page 42) out to the edge of the module to get Ornamental Ball Module.

x12 = CUBOCTAHEDRON
x24 = RHOMBICUBOCTAHEDRON

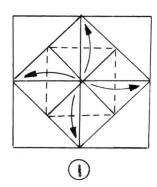

①

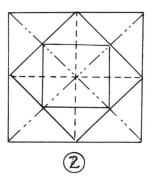

②

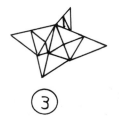

③

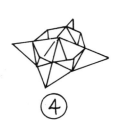

④

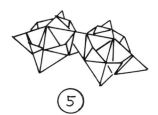

⑤

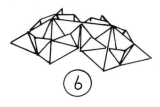

⑥

x12

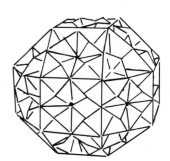

x24

44

Simple Square Module by Bennett Arnstein

Square analog of One-Piece Triangle Module (page 37),
Assembles like Spike Ball Module (page 42)

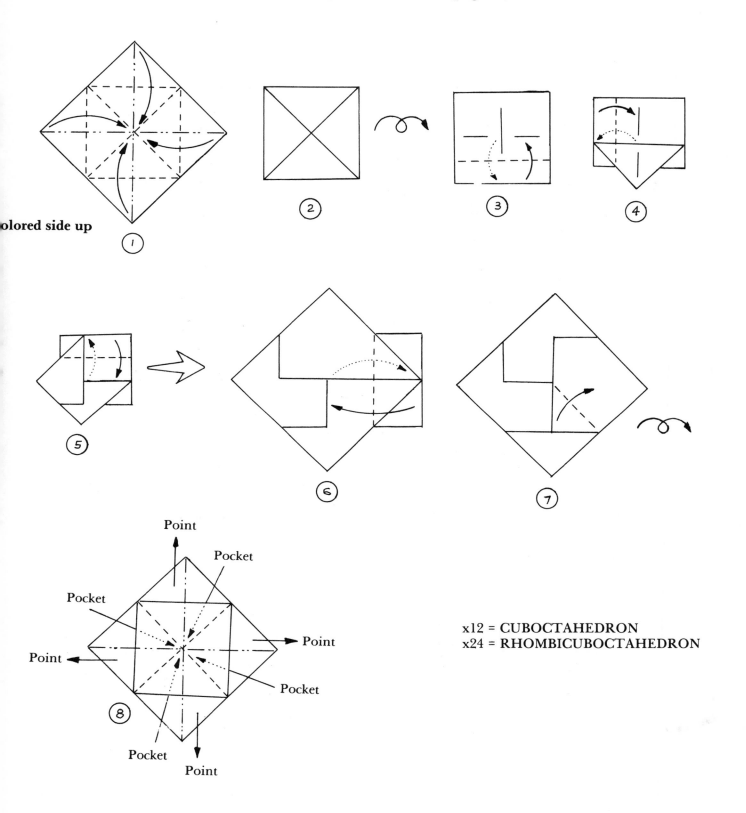

colored side up

Point

Pocket

Pocket

Point

Point

Pocket

Pocket

Point

x12 = CUBOCTAHEDRON
x24 = RHOMBICUBOCTAHEDRON

Three-Loop Cuboctahedron by Rona Gurkewitz

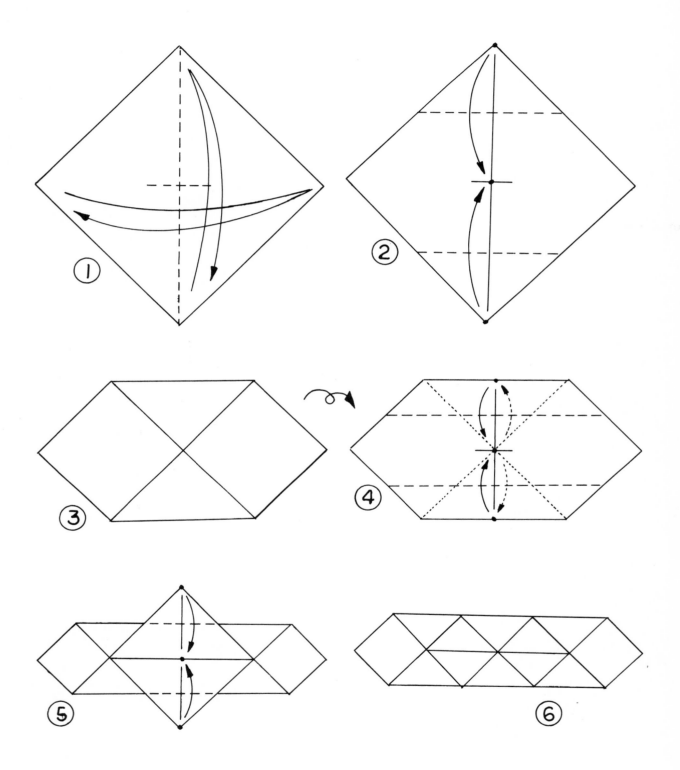

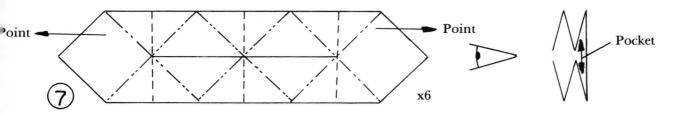

Point ← ... → Point

x6

Pocket

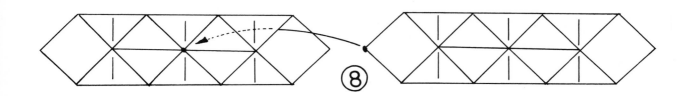

(7)

(8)

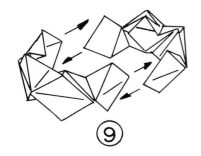

(9)

(10)

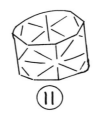

(11)

(12)

(13)

(14)

Equilateral Triangle Module Systems

Equilateral Triangle Strip System I
by Lewis Simon and Bennett Arnstein

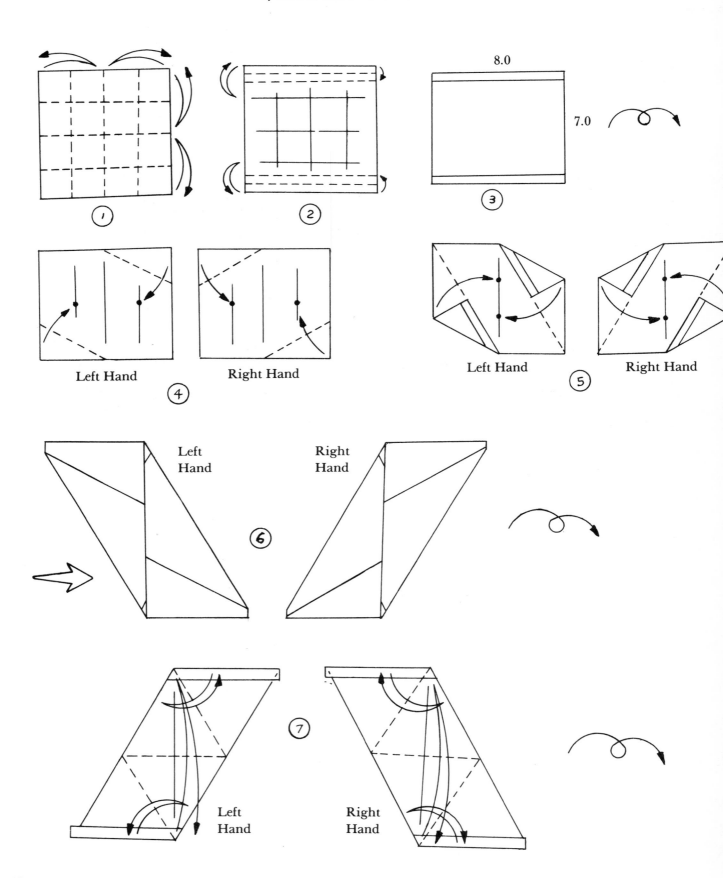

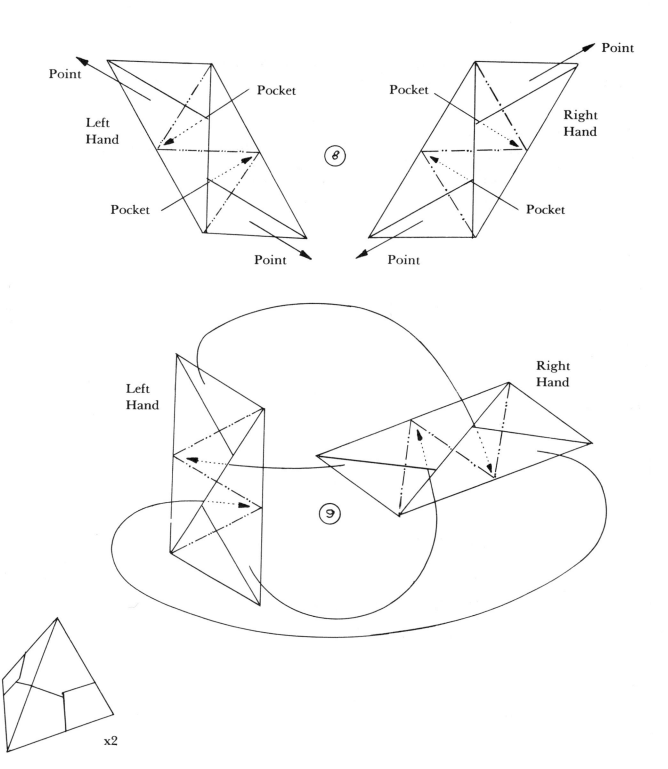

Models from one type of module:
x2 = TETRAHEDRON
x3 = DOUBLE TETRAHEDRON
x4 = OCTAHEDRON
x5 = DOUBLE PENTAGONAL PYRAMID
x6 = EQUILATERAL TRIANGLE DODECAHEDRON
x12 = STELLATED OCTAHEDRON
x12 = STELLATED CUBE
x30 = STELLATED DODECAHEDRON 1
x30 = STELLATED DODECAHEDRON 2 *
x30 = DIMPLED DODECAHEDRON

from right and left
1r,1l = TETRAHEDRON
3r,3l = DIAMOND HEXAHEDRON
4r,4l = HEXADECAHEDRON
5r,5l = ICOSAHEDRON

*Adhesives and internal stiffening (pasting shaped pieces of construction paper to the interior *faces* of a model) required.

Equilateral Triangle Strip System II
by Lewis Simon and Bennett Arnstein

This module has the same model-making possibilities as the Equilateral Triangle Strip System I. The main difference is that this module starts with a 2 by 1 paper. There are left- and right-handed versions of this module as well. Only the left-handed module is shown in these diagrams. See the other diagrams for making a right-handed module (next model).

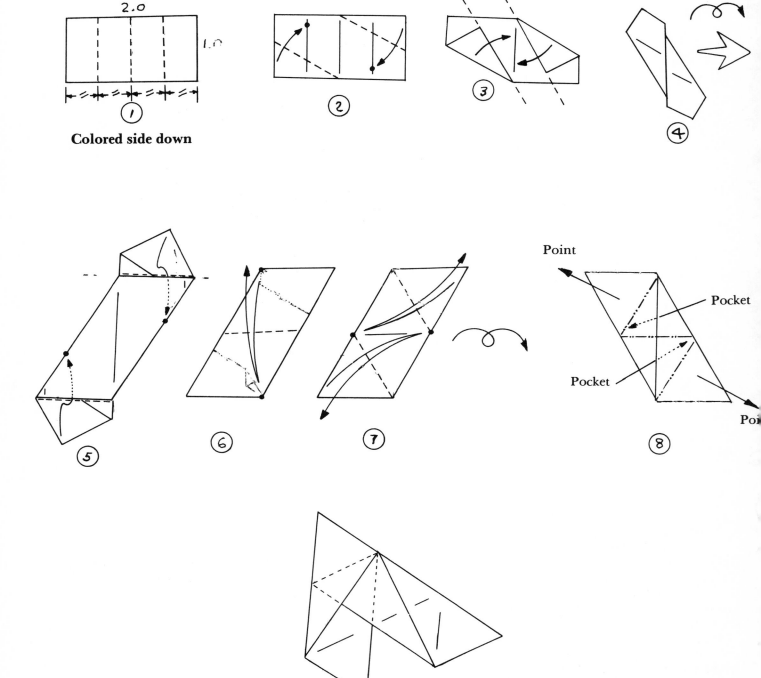

Colored side down

10-Module Icosahedron from Equilateral Triangle Strip
System I or II
by Bennett Arnstein

Make 5 right-hand and 5 left-hand modules. Join the five left-handed modules together with glue or tape on the inside to form a five-sided pyramid. Repeat this process with the five right-handed modules. One pyramid becomes the north pole and the other pyramid the south pole. The belt around the equator is formed by inserting the remaining points on each pyramid into the remaining pockets on the other pyramid. Use glue on the first four connections of the equatorial belt. The remaining connections may be made without any adhesive. This model is attractive when folded from paper with different colors on each side.

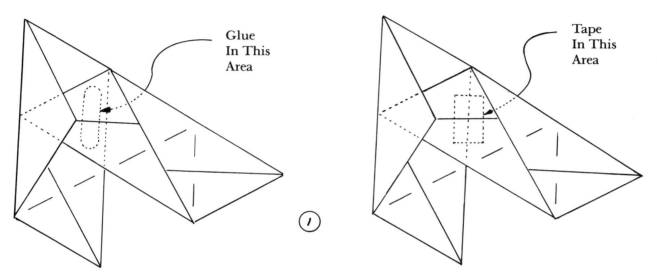

Glue In This Area

Tape In This Area

Left-Handed Modules Shown Above

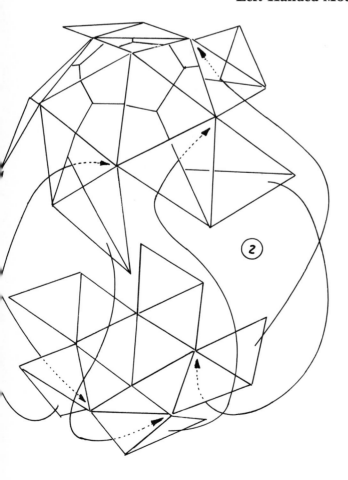

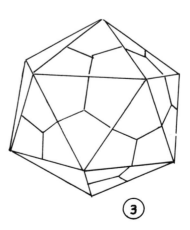

Miscellaneous Models

These models are made from the Equilateral Triangle Strip System I or II. Half the modules are left-handed and half are right-handed. The assembly procedure is similar to that used in the 10-module icosahedron. The left-handed modules form a pyramid at the north pole and the right-handed modules form a pyramid at the south pole. The remaining points on each pyramid are inserted into the remaining pockets on the other pyramid to form a belt around the equator. If locking tabs are used in assembling the pyramids, neither of these models will need any glue. If locking tabs are not used, a small amount of glue will be needed to assemble the four module pyramids.

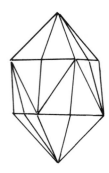

8-Module Hexadecahedron   **6-Module Diamond Hexahedron**

Triangle Edge Module
by Lewis Simon and Bennett Arnstein

Unfold mountain crease made in FIG. 1. Crease A on entering module lines up with crease B on receiving module. Crease B on entering module lines up with mountain crease along diagonal seam on receiving module. This module makes polyhedra with flat equilateral triangle faces. The module corresponds to an edge of the polyhedron. Most polyhedra will require the use of the lock tab. If it is not needed, fold it flat against the point tab.

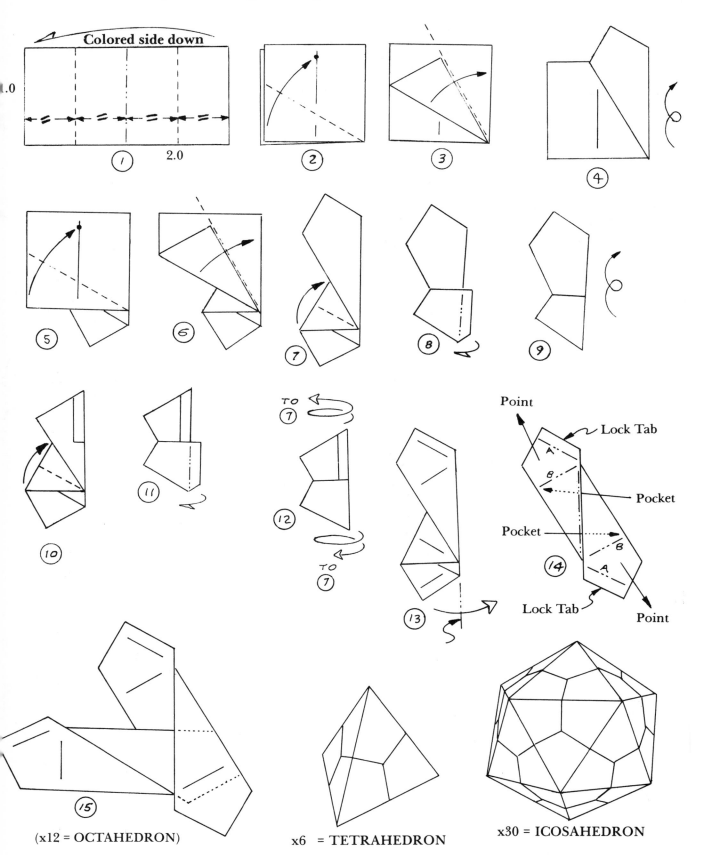

(x12 = OCTAHEDRON)

x6 = TETRAHEDRON

x30 = ICOSAHEDRON

53

Stellation Module Systems

36-Degree Isosceles Triangle Module by Bennett Arnstein

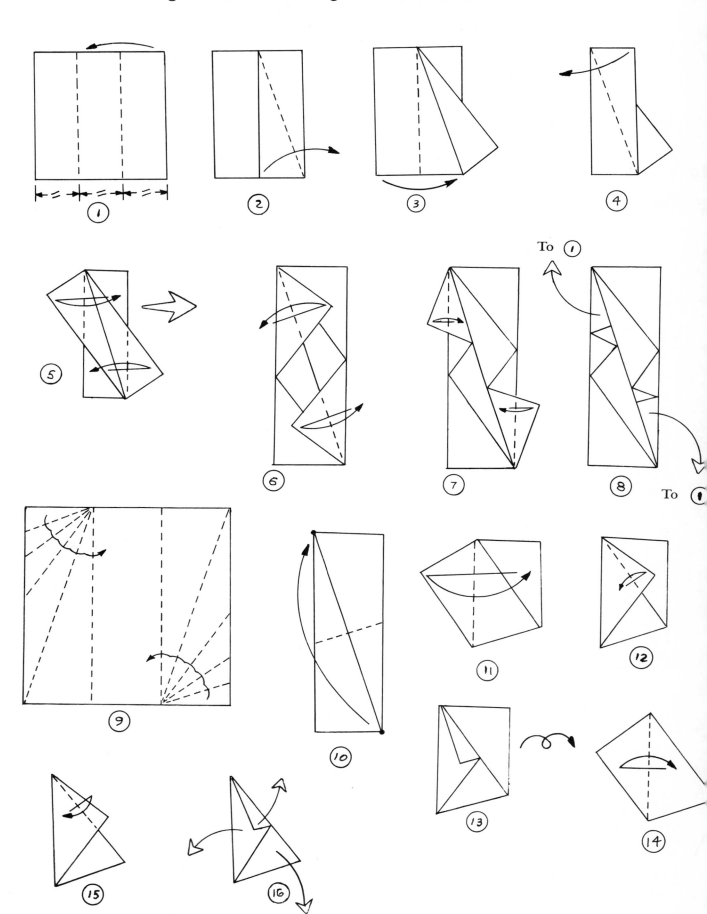

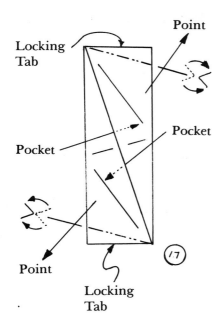

Point

Locking
Tab

Pocket

Pocket

Point

Locking
Tab

⑰

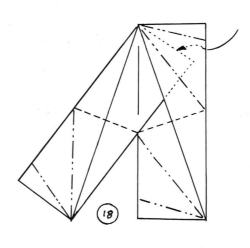

⑱

Locking tab on *entering
module* gets bent around
mountain crease on *re-
ceiving module*

3 modules make a triangular pyramid.
4 modules make a square pyramid.
5 modules make a pentagonal pyramid.

x6 = STELLATED TETRAHEDRON
x12 = STELLATED CUBE*
x12 = STELLATED OCTAHEDRON
x30 = STELLATED DODECAHEDRON 1
x30 = STELLATED DODECAHEDRON 2*

No adhesive is needed to make triangular pyramids. However, a small amount is necessary to make square or pentagonal pyramids.

*Adhesives and internal stiffening (pasting shaped pieces of construction paper to the interior *faces* of a model) required.

45-Degree Isosceles Stellation Module by Rona Gurkewitz

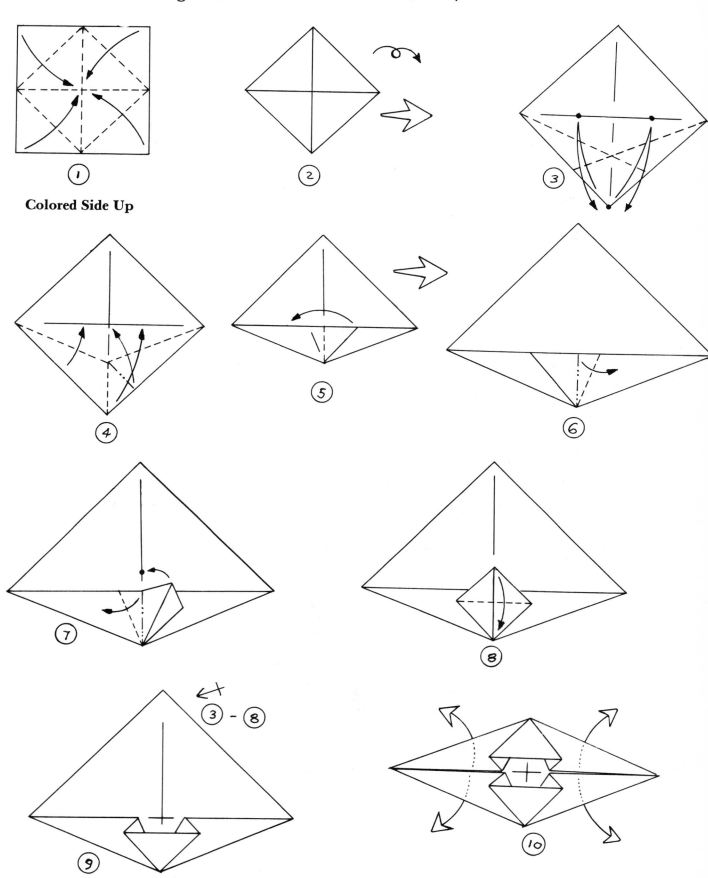

Colored Side Up

56

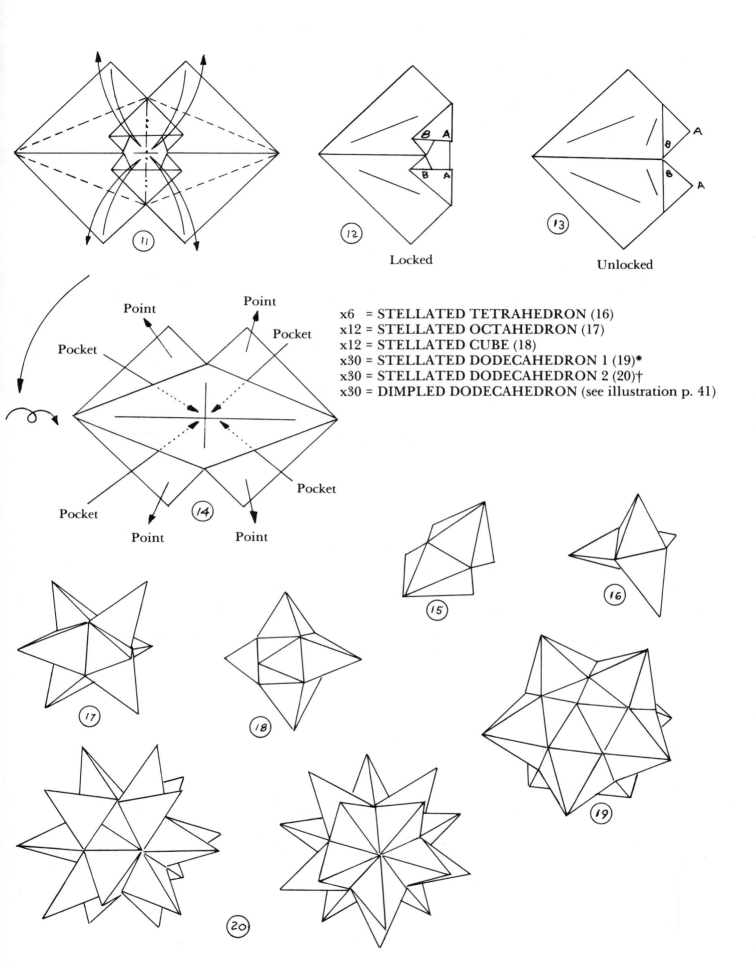

Locked

Unlocked

Point   Point

Pocket

Pocket

Pocket

Pocket

Point   Point

x6 = **STELLATED TETRAHEDRON** (16)
x12 = **STELLATED OCTAHEDRON** (17)
x12 = **STELLATED CUBE** (18)
x30 = **STELLATED DODECAHEDRON 1** (19)*
x30 = **STELLATED DODECAHEDRON 2** (20)†
x30 = **DIMPLED DODECAHEDRON** (see illustration p. 41)

Adhesives and internal stiffening (pasting shaped pieces of construction paper to the interior *faces* of a model) required.
Adhesives required.

Great Dodecahedron Systems

Pentagon Module: Great Dodecahedron by Bennett Arnstein

Pentagon analog of One-Piece Triangle Module (page 37).
x12 = GREAT DODECAHEDRON.

Colored side up

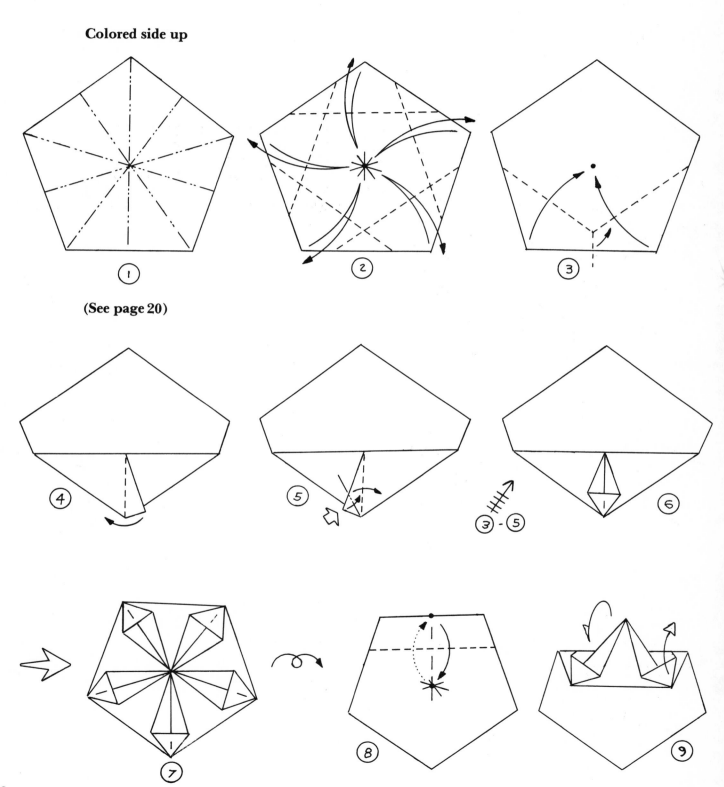

(See page 20)

58

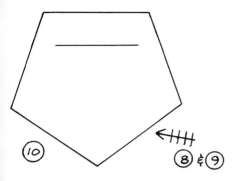

⑩ ⟵HHH ⑧ & ⑨

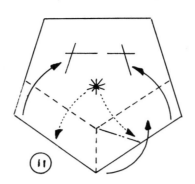

⑪

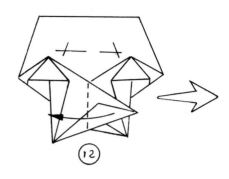

⑫

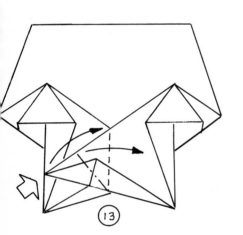

⑬

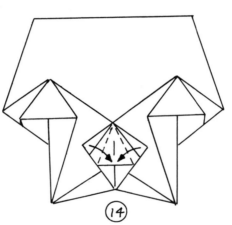

⑭

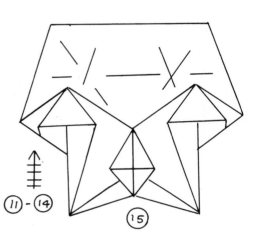

⑪ - ⑭   ⑮

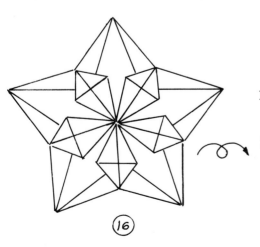

⑯

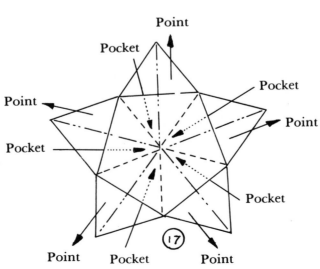

Point

Pocket

Pocket

Point

Point

Pocket

Pocket

Point   Pocket   Point

⑰

59

Simplified Pentagon Module: Great Dodecahedron
by Bennett Arnstein

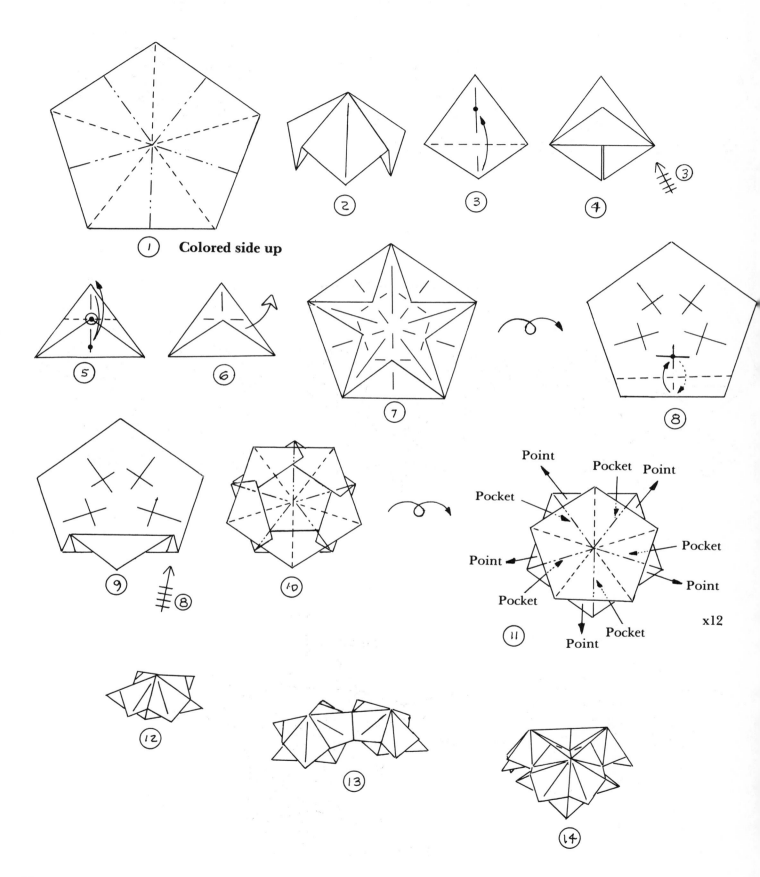

1. Colored side up

11. Point Pocket Point Pocket Pocket Point Point Pocket Point Pocket Point x12

12-Module Great Dodecahedron by Bennett Arnstein

Pentagon module based on Rona Gurkewitz's Spike Ball Module

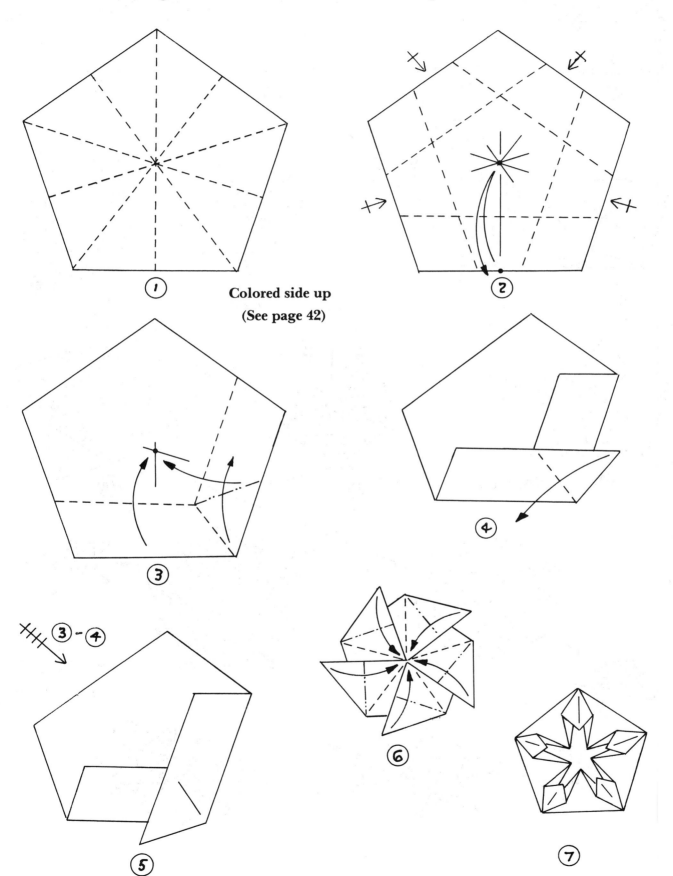

Colored side up

(See page 42)

①

②

③

④

③–④

⑤

⑥

⑦

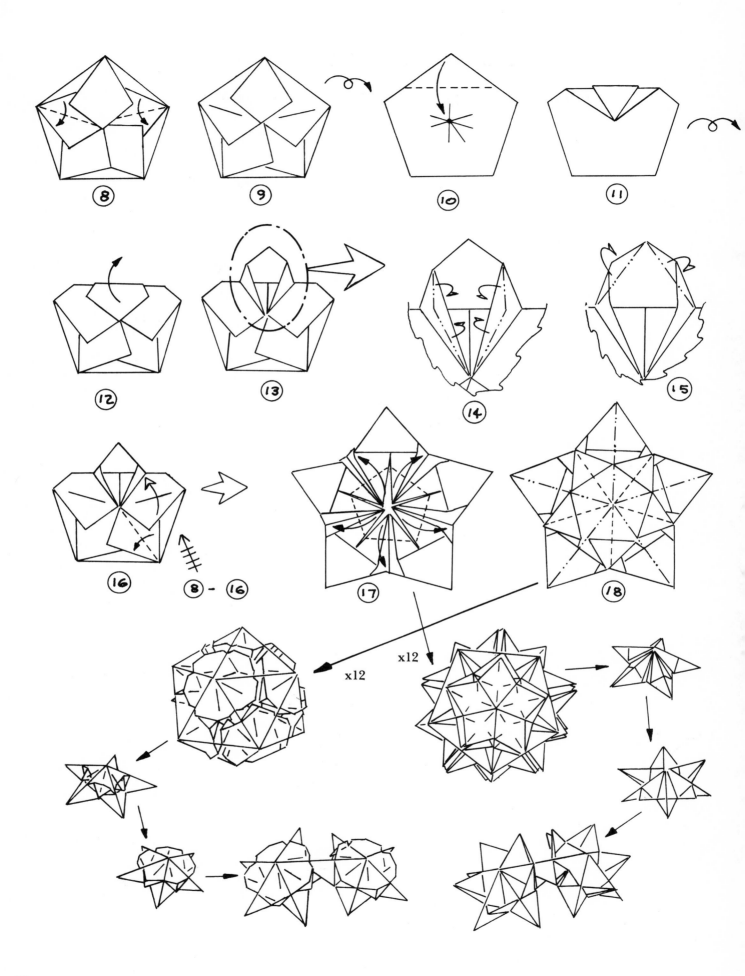

Flat Patterns from Equilateral Triangle Tessellations*

Flat Patterns That Can Be Laid Out on an Equilateral Triangle Tessellation

Note: The models in this Flat Patterns section are not, of course, true origami. They are supplied here as three-dimensional objects which are *suggested* by the modules in this book but which the authors have been unable to complete *as* modular origami. These workable patterns may be treated as a challenge to the enthusiast, since they represent unsolved problems in geometric modular origami.

⊙ **Designates the North Pole of Each Solid**

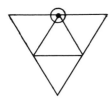

Tetrahedron

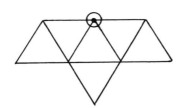

Double Tetrahedron

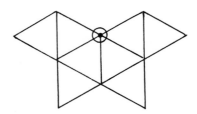

Octahedron

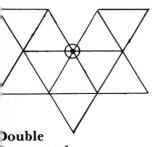

Double Pentagonal Pyramid

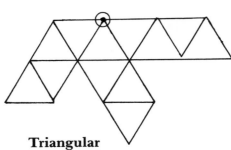

Triangular Dodecahedron

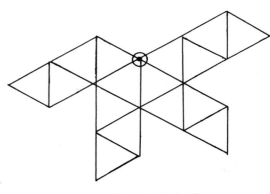

Hexadecahedron

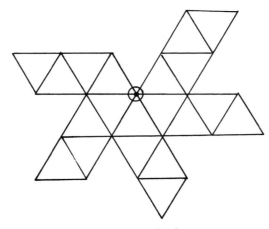

Icosahedron

Stellations of these modules may be built using the Equilateral Triangle Strip Module I (page 48) to form tetrahedron pyramids; or the 45-Degree Isosceles Stellation Module (page 56) to form 45-degree triangle pyramids; or the 36-Degree Isosceles Triangle Module (page 54) to form 36-degree triangle pyramids.

*Tabs may be added to all the flat patterns to allow assembly of the solids with glue.

Truncated Hexadecahedron Flat Pattern

Truncated Hexadecahedron

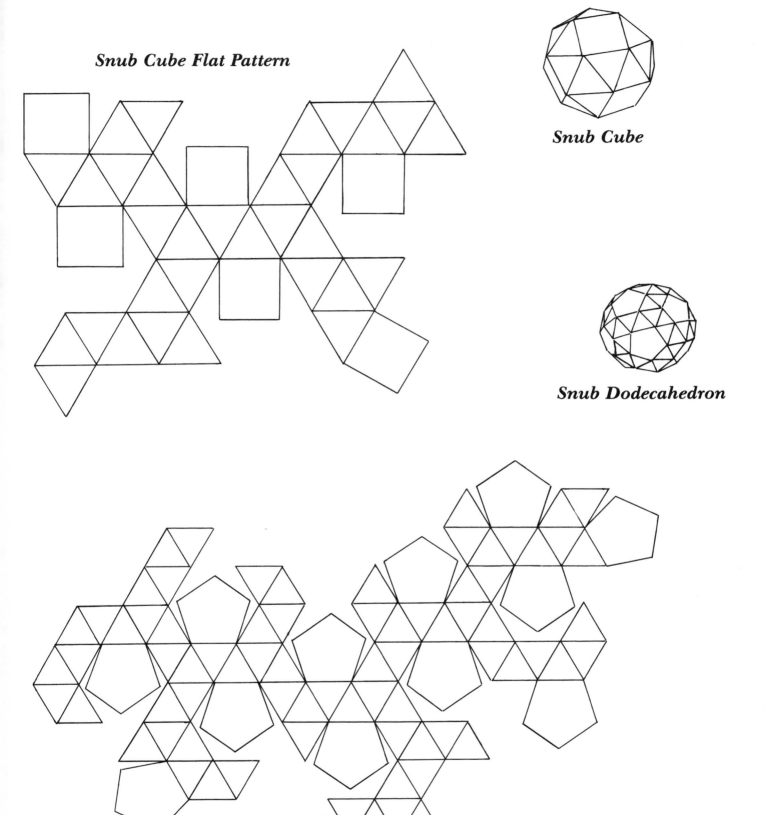

Snub Cube Flat Pattern

Snub Cube

Snub Dodecahedron

Snub Dodecahedron Flat Pattern

Supplementary Material

(Clockwise)
Truncated icosahedron
Truncated hexadecahedron
Dodecahedron
(All composed of One-Piece Triangle modules, page 37)

Finding Models in the Book: Index by Polyhedron

Books of Related Interest

Cundy and Rollett, *Mathematical Models,* Oxford University Press, London, New York, 1961

Senechal and Fleck, eds., *Shaping Space, A Polyhedral Approach,* Birkhauser, Boston, 1988

Simon and Arnstein, *Modular Origami Polyhedra,* Bennett Arnstein, 1989 (ISBN 0-9620058-1-9)

Wenninger, *Polyhedron Models,* Cambridge University Press, New York, London, 1974.

Wenninger, *Polyhedron Models for the Classroom,* 1975, National Council of Teachers of Mathematics, 1906 Association Drive, Reston, Virginia 22091

Finding Other Folders

There are many local groups in the U.S. that have meetings at which people get together to improve their folding. There also are international groups. Some of these groups have conventions and/or newsletters. If you have a computer, you can communicate with other folders through the Internet.

Internet Discussion Group and World Wide Web

To access origami discussion by computer you will need a way of accessing the Internet. This can be done through an on-line service such as Compuserve, a service provider, or a school, university or workplace, with modern computer and communications software. Once on the net you can get subscription information by sending a message to:

maarten@info.service.rug.nl

The body of the message is "faq" (frequently asked questions). Discussions range over many topics including books, folds, mathematical origami and conventions. There is an archive site at rugcis.rug.nl which has all messages as well as articles, photos and more.

If you have access to the World Wide Web part of the internet, there are a number of origami home pages there. Joseph Wu's page, which has been featured as a Cool Page of the Week, can be found at:

http://www.cs.ubc.ca/spider/jwu/origami.html.

Origami Organizations

The largest North American origami organization is Origami U.S.A. (formerly known as F.O.C.A.). It has a newsletter, an annual convention and special sessions throughout the year. It also has a mail-order operation featuring a large selection of origami books and paper. To find out about O.U.S.A. send a S.A.S.E. with two first-class stamps to 15 W. 77 St., N.Y., N.Y. 10024. It can also provide you with information about origami organizations all over the world.

About the Authors

Rona Gurkewitz is an Associate Professor of Mathematics and Computer Science at Western Connecticut State University. She became interested in origami in 1972 after meeting Laura Kruskal and Lillian Oppenheimer. Laura Kruskal is a creative folder and teacher and Lillian Oppenheimer was the founder of the Origami Center of America and was the International First Lady of Paperfolding during her lifetime.

A couple of years later, Rona became interested in polyhedra through a math education class taught by her colleague Stacey Wahl. Rona set about combining these two interests, and has shared geometric paper-folds with math teachers and others ever since. She has taught many classes, has had her work exhibited and has had folds published. She was a founding member of the Friends of the Origami Center of America (now called Origami U.S.A.) and served on its Board of Directors for five years.

Bennett Arnstein has been a mechanical-hardware engineer in the aerospace industry for over twenty years. He holds four patents. He became interested in polyhedra when he was ten years old. He has written three books, two of them on origami and polyhedra. One of these books was written with Lewis Simon, an eminent geometric designer and folder and a tremendous influence on Bennett. Bennett is a member of Origami U.S.A. and the West Coast Origami Guild and is a frequent contributor to their newsletters. He has done much teaching and exhibiting, as well as designing and folding origami models.